COME
AND SEE

COME
AND SEE

STEPPING INTO THE NOW OF GOD

JOEL BUTZ

Cover design: Ariel Butz
Editing: Regina McCollam
Editing and Interior layout: Creatively Inspired, LLC,
creativelyinspiredlife.com

Printed in the United States of America

CONTENTS

Death | 115
Enough | 119
Prosperity | 123
Exceeding | 129
Ergonomics | 135
Faithful | 139
Father | 143
Us | 147
Mercy | 151
Grace | 157
Healing | 161
Hope | 169
Glory | 173
Kedging | 177
Now | 181
Legacy | 187
Monsters | 191
Rules | 195
Sadness | 201
Temptations | 203
Vanity | 209
Yes | 213

End Notes | 217

Death	115
Enough	119
Prosperity	123
Exceeding	129
Ergonomics	135
Faithful	139
Father	143
Us	147
Mercy	151
Grace	157
Healing	161
Hope	169
Glory	173
Kedging	177
Now	181
Legacy	187
Monsters	191
Rules	195
Sadness	201
Temptations	203
Vanity	209
Yes	213
End Notes	217

ACKNOWLEDGEMENTS

My thanks to—

- Regina McCollam and Carol Cantrell, for pulling this all together.

- Von B, for teaching me to bend.

- Tom P, for showing where to find the Easter eggs.

FOREWORD

I ran across the following quote one day that has since captivated my attention. It's from that great theologian, Dr. Seuss—you know, the author of such landmark spiritual writings as, *Green Eggs and Ham*, and *How the Grinch Stole Christmas*. He said:

> *You know you're in love when you don't want to go to sleep because your reality has become greater than your dreams.*

One of the reasons this quote has so fascinated me is its challenge to my thinking that "If it's that good, it must be too good to be true." It has also forced me to ask the questions: Is there a greater reality than I am presently experiencing and have I settled for the less, when the more is not only possible, but available? Is it possible that the children's poet and illustrator of *The Cat in The Hat* has a better understanding of Ephesians 3:20 than I do?

> *Now to Him who is able to do exceedingly, abundantly, above all we could ask or think, according to the power that lives in you.*

I have come to believe that Dr. Seuss has put into poetry as a possibility what Paul put in sacred Scripture as a reality. The truth of a greater reality is the resounding declaration that weaves throughout this powerful book, Come and See, written by my dear friend and colleague.

Allow me a personal illustration of the exceeding abundance into which we have been invited. A few weeks following a devastating loss, my wife Deborah and I took some time away in Hawaii to recover and find our footing. It was a vacation we already had on the calendar and came at an opportune time. However, because of what we were going through, we decided to go five days earlier than scheduled. I searched the Internet to find a condo that would be available at such short notice, and was encouraged to find one in a resort we had used before. I booked the least expensive villa, one tucked up in the golf course with a "fairway view." When we arrived to check in to the villa, the receptionist informed us that they had upgraded us to a "Gold" villa—a unit that had been completely renovated and updated. We were thankful for the upgrade, and upon entering the villa we became very excited about the beautiful and inviting accommodations. Even the view of the golf course in the foreground and the Pacific Ocean on the horizon was more than we expected.

We unpacked our clothes and had just settled into the comfortable living room furniture to read when the phone rang. It was the front desk. The receptionist who had welcomed us upon our arrival came quickly to the point of her call.

"Mr. Crone, we would like to upgrade you to an Ocean View Villa." Though this sounded good, it was late and we were tired from the trip. Besides, we were quite happy with the condo we were now settled into. My response was simply, "I'll talk to my wife and call you back." After talking with Deb, we agreed that we were content and were choosing to remain in our present condo.

When I called the receptionist back and gave her our answer, her response surprised me, "Will you at least let us show you a couple of units, and then you can decide?"

Being an extensive traveler, I'm always interested in upgrades, so I agreed. Though Deb was not very interested, she decided to go along anyway, and a few minutes later, a van showed up at our door. A very polite young man took us down near the ocean and showed us a couple of units with ocean views. Though they had beautiful views, it was obvious that the units were not "Gold" units. The furnishings in the living rooms were very sparse and uncomfortable, and at this point in our journey, we needed somewhere we could be comfortable. We returned to our original unit, called the front desk, thanked the receptionist for the offer but informed her we would stay where we were. Again, her response surprised me, and this time raised my suspicion that something was up.

"Will you let us show you some more units that have the furnishings you're looking for?"

My curiosity and suspicion got the best of me and I said, "Obviously you have a problem and need us to help you resolve it. Is that right?"

"Yes," she said. She went on to explain that the owner of the unit we were occupying had unexpectedly arrived and was demanding the use of his own condo. No matter how much the receptionist explained the situation, the owner continued to insist on being placed in his condo. As we finally understood the true situation, Deb and I let her know that if she could find a unit comparable in comfort to the one we were presently in, no matter where it was located, we would be willing to make a move. The receptionist was greatly relieved and promised to find such a unit and provide help for us to move our luggage. While she looked for another unit, we repacked our suitcases. It was now about 8:00 P.M. Hawaii time, 11:00 P.M. West Coast time where we had just come from. We were exhausted.

It wasn't long until the van pulled up, and a pleasant woman greeted us, helped us carry our luggage to the van, and transported us down to the ocean front condos that lined the bay. When we stepped into the unit, we were immediately overwhelmed. To say that this was a "Gold" unit would be an understatement. The unit set right above the beach and the entire front of the condo, kitchen, dining room and living room, had a panoramic view of the Pacific Ocean, the majestic Fleming Beach, and the beautiful Honolua Bay. The beach was a one-minute walk from the front door. The furnishings of this ocean front condo were stunning in both quality and comfort. Everything about it was first class and luxurious. It was exceedingly, abundantly, above and beyond what we could ask or even think to ask. That astonishing upgrade was the first of the Father's expressions of love and goodness that filled the days to follow. He was inviting us to "Come and See," though His voice sounded just a bit like the receptionist's . . . insistent with invitations to just look.

This book, *Come and See*, is for the adventurer—the person unwilling to settle for their present reality and willing to step into the unknown. Joel does not allow you to put your mind in neutral. On the contrary, *Come and See* will challenge many of your present mindsets. However, he presents the reader with many *selah* opportunities in which you can release yourself into the love of God, and be out of your mind, luxuriating in His goodness.

As you read this book, hear the invitation of the Holy Spirit to experience the more that is available in every part, and every occurrence of your life. Read it with the expectation that you will encounter the God of the greater reality. He will not disappoint you.

Is He too good to be true? Come and see.

—David Crone
Sr. Leader of The Mission in Vacaville, CA
Author of *Prisoner of Hope, The Power of Your Life Message, Declarations That Empower Us,* and *Decisions That Define Us.*

COME AND SEE

"We have found the one Moses wrote about in the Law, and about whom the prophets also wrote— Jesus of Nazareth, the son of Joseph."

"Nazareth! Can anything good come from there?" Nathanael asked.

"Come and see," said Philip.

John 1:45, 46

t's time to reintroduce an old thought—God brings good things from bad places.

Philip's question is a reasonable one and stands as a metaphor for all of our questions today.

"My daughter is in ICU." Can anything good come out of Nazareth?

"I have cancer." Can anything good come out of Nazareth?

"I just lost my baby." Can anything good come out of Nazareth?

"I just lost my job." Can anything good come out of Nazareth?

"I was in a car accident (again)." Can anything good come out of Nazareth?

You get the idea. We live in a broken world that is full of suffering, and we all have these places in our lives that we look at and ask, "Can anything good come from there?" The Christmas story answers this question for us with a resounding, "Yes".

Look at these excerpts from Matthew's genealogy of Jesus:

- Judah the father of Perez and Zerah, whose mother was Tamar;

- Salmon the father of Boaz, whose mother was Rahab;

- Boaz the father of Obed, whose mother was Ruth;

- David was the father of Solomon, whose mother had been Uriah's wife;

- Manasseh the father of Amon;

- Josiah, the father of Jeconiah, and his brothers at the time of the exile to Babylon.

After the exile to Babylon, the genealogy continues—

Jacob the father of Joseph, the husband of Mary, and Mary was the mother of Jesus who is called the Messiah.

Now look again.

Tamar was a barren widow. The men she slept with died. She got pregnant by pretending to be a hooker and having sex with her father-in-law. Can anything good come out of a barren widowed incestuous relationship?

Rahab was a prostitute and a foreigner. Can anything good come out of a foreign prostitute?

Ruth was from Moab. Can anything good come out of Moab, this land that has been so hostile towards Israel?

Uriah's wife isn't even named by Matthew; she's just the wife of the man David had killed in order to cover up their adultery after she got pregnant. Can anything good come out of an adulterous, murderous love-triangle?

Look at the life of Manasseh, a king of Israel:

Manasseh practiced soothsaying, used witchcraft and sorcery, and consulted mediums and spiritists. He did much evil in the sight of the LORD, to provoke Him to anger. He even set a carved image, the idol which he had made, in the house of God.

2 Chronicles 33:5

Manasseh's son, Amon, worshipped all of the idols his father set up. Can anything good come out of a king who reinstates child sacrifice and actually sets up an idol in the place God was to be worshipped?

Then there is the exile to Babylon. Can anything come out of brutal torture, enslavement, and death?

And finally there is Joseph and Mary. Can anything good come from this unexpected and out-of-wedlock pregnancy?

Jesus' genealogical history is anything but pristine. But ultimately this is the message of the Christmas story; when God is telling the story, our history need not determine our destiny. God can redeem any person in any situation at any time in any place. Yes, something good can come from Nazareth. But here is where we need to make a change.

If Nathaniel asks the question of the ages, "Can anything good come from Nazareth?" then Philip gives us the answer of the ages, "Come and see."

"Come and see," is the answer to all of our questions. Why? Because redemption is a process, not a moment.

The answer to "Can anything good come out of _____?" (fill in the blank with your current crisis) will not be found in a moment, but in a process where, by faith, you continually come to Jesus and see what He is doing. Jesus is the answer to life's question, "Can anything good come from there?"

So in whatever season of life you are in, may you gather up all of your pain, all of your questions, all of your confusion, all of your Nazareths, and just come and see what the Lord has done. Come and see what the Lord is doing. Come and see what He will do. There is a NOW-ness to the Kingdom of God that we need to lay hold of.

We all have a Nazareth in our lives. Can anything good come from there?

Just come and see.

TREASURE

The kingdom of heaven is like treasure buried in a field that a man found and reburied. Then in his, joy he goes and sells everything he has and buys that field.

Matthew 13:44

I am sure you are all familiar with this parable as an expression of the value of the Kingdom of God; it is worth selling everything we have in this world to gain. This is true. But I think there is more going on in this parable, and I'll tell you why. Even if I were to sell everything I had, and everything you had, and everything everyone else had, it still would not be enough to buy the field. So I ask myself, "What else is happening in this story? Who else could pay this kind of price?" Then the little child in me starts jumping up and down saying, "I know! I know! Jesus can!" That's where I begin seeing this parable with new eyes: I am the field; Jesus is the man.

I think this is a parable that stretches all the way back to the Garden of Eden. What is a field made of? Dirt. What did God form the first human from? Dirt. Adam was literally God's field. Adam was God's garden, which God would personally tend with the expectation that the dirt creature, "the groundling" as some translate the Hebrew word, *ha-adamah*, would yield to God's care and bear much fruit. At the same time, God planted a garden in the earth and put the human there to tend it, as a parable of the relationship between God and human; as the human tended the garden and it produced fruit, so God would tend the human and we would produce fruit. However, because of sin, God's field would now bear thorns and thistles in response to God's attempt to tend it. In parallel, God decreed that man's field would bear thorns and thistles in response to man's attempt to tend it.

But God does not leave the story there. Jesus comes to earth as the embodiment of God's eternal love. He looks past the state of our field and somehow, because love hopes all things and love believes all things, Jesus sees treasure in the field of me and in the field of you. Some of us may have lain fallow; some of us may have lain desolate; some of us may have even been producing some meager fruit. In any case, the state of the field is irrelevant to the story. Jesus is not evaluating the quality of the field; He is looking for the treasure that lies beneath. In joy at His discovery, Jesus gave everything He had to buy the field of me and the field of you. The joy that was set before Him by which He endured the cross, was, I believe at least in part, the anticipation of returning to the fields of men and, with His own hand, unearthing the treasure that only He could see.

This is where I find myself in God's story. I have been bought with a price, redeemed by the precious blood of Jesus. He has marked me for His own. I am His treasured possession,

His field, His garden. Slowly but surely, the treasure that He saw in me so long ago is now being revealed.

And so it is with you.

Take heart.

VISION

All fruitfulness is grounded in vision. Fruitfulness depends upon our ability to see that good can come from bad, that God can produce pearls from our pain. God wants to establish heavenly vision in His people, but here in America, there are three spirits that are waging war against God's purpose. To embrace these spirits is to lose vision. To embrace these spirits is to deny our destiny and to deny our obligation to take our places as sons and daughters in the Kingdom of God. And so, we must confront these spirits in ourselves.

First, there is an orphan spirit at work. This spirit envies the wealthy, it covets their wealth, and it desires that all things be reduced to the level of its own vision. This spirit has no honor for the sacrifices of previous generations and no vision for future generations. It is a prodigal spirit that denies the sufficiency of a father's love and seeks only to possess the wealth of others for the sake of its own immediate pleasures. Envy often wears the deceitful mask of justice. However, God's justice is neither covetous nor contentious, but always seeks the restoration of relationships as its primary ethic. The prophet Malachi said that in the last days, Elijah would come and turn the hearts of the fathers to the children and the hearts of the children to the fathers. The enemy cannot allow this, so he is working now to turn the hearts of one generation against the hearts of another generation by causing the children to envy and covet the wealth of the fathers, while the fathers, in turn, hide their wealth from the children. This is wrong and it must stop. We who walk daily in the mercies of God must silence the voice that says, "It's not fair," because to embrace this voice is to embrace envy. The Kingdom of God is not about fairness; it is about mercy. We who have received mercy must choose to walk in a daily gratitude for that mercy rather than in a resentful envy of those who are wealthy in this world. We must choose to embrace mercy over "fairness" because these two things cannot coexist in the Kingdom of God.

Second, there is a spirit of fear at work. This spirit is primarily about fear of loss: loss of power, loss of wealth, loss of freedom, and loss of voice. It wants to build walls, to hoard, to protect, and to turn away from others in need. It believes that life is a zero sum game, and that to make room for another means the loss of part of oneself. It seeks to blind us to the reality of God's kingdom.

"Seek first the Kingdom of God," Jesus said, "and all of these things will be added to you."[1] God's kingdom is about addition, not subtraction. Yet the fear of loss prevents us from reaching out towards the other as the embodied presence of God, not realizing that as we cut ourselves off from the other, we also cut ourselves off from the economy of the God who promised to supply all of our needs according to His riches in glory.[2] This is wrong and it must stop. We have an obligation as sons and daughters of the King to spend ourselves for the sake of the other. We must choose to embrace grace over fear, because these two things cannot coexist in the Kingdom of God.

Third, there is a spirit of division. This is a spirit that works closely with the other two. It seeks to divide and conquer. This spirit works constantly to bring division between male and female, between homosexual and heterosexual, between black and white, between Muslim and Christian, between the haves and those who have less, between enemies of God and friends of God, between the new immigrants and those who seem to have forgotten that scarcely a handful of generations ago, their families were the immigrants. By dividing people into groups and pitting groups against one another, this spirit seeks power over all. This is wrong and it must stop.

The Kingdom of God is not about division, but about multiplication. Jesus broke all dividing walls on the cross. God was in Christ reconciling the world to Himself, so that while we were all still sinners, and all still enemies of God, Christ died for us all.[3] In that single action, Christ reduced all of humanity to a single fundamental category: those for whom He died. We have an obligation now as ministers of reconciliation to reject any tendency to categorize people. Instead, we must embrace every person simply as one for whom Christ died. We must choose to embrace reconciliation over division because these two things cannot coexist in the Kingdom of God.

So how do we overcome the activities of these three spirits, which are warring against God's purposes?

We repent, and we receive.

The first weapon of our warfare is repentance, both personal and incarnational. We must personally root out and repent of any sense of envy, fear, or divisiveness/control because these things prevent the renewing of our minds, and they destroy vision. We must corporately relearn the role of incarnational repentance. The prophet Daniel was one of the most righteous men in the Bible, yet he repented as one with the people—"We have sinned. . . ."[4] Intercession that speaks of "they" or "them" is already falling into the embrace of at least one of three evil spirits. Intercession must begin in repentance, and repentance must begin with "we." What we see, then, from Daniel's example is that the moment Daniel set himself to repent, an angel was sent from God to bring him one thing—vision. Repentance releases heavenly messengers with heavenly vision. Repentance is the key to vision.

Next we must be intentional about receiving the Holy Spirit in three different ways.

We must receive the Holy Spirit as the Spirit of adoption. Paul wrote that we did not receive a spirit that makes us slaves to fear, but we received the Spirit of adoption.[5] So now we can displace the orphan spirit with its envy of others by daily welcoming the Holy Spirit as the Spirit of adoption who is always in us empowering us to say, "Our Father."

We must receive the Holy Spirit as the Spirit of revelation. Paul wrote that we did not receive the spirit of this world but we received the Spirit who is from God so that we may understand what has freely been given to us by God. So now we can displace the fear of loss by listening daily to the voice of the Holy Spirit who is constantly revealing what has already been given to us, and constantly speaking to us about what is to come.[6]

We must receive the Holy Spirit as the Spirit of power, love, and of a sound mind. Paul wrote that we did not receive a spirit of fearfulness, literally, "timidity" but of power, love, and of a sound mind.[7] So now we can displace the desire to divide in order to control by receiving from the Holy Spirit the power to speak boldly, the hope that does not disappoint (because God's love has been poured into our hearts[8]), and the mind of Christ[9] so that we might be faithful managers of the mysteries of God.[10]

Vision is not just for us. The word "managers" in 1 Corinthians 4:1 is *oikonomous*, from which we get the word, "economy." Follow me for a moment. Fruitfulness is grounded in vision. Repentance is the key to vision. Vision is the key to God's economy. God's economy was first revealed to Abraham as "all the peoples on earth will be blessed through you." The church is supposed to be in the business of managing God's economy for the sake of the world.

Imagine with me what it would look like if the church in America were to reject the orphan spirit and embrace the spirit of adoption. What would it look like if the church in America were to reject the spirit of fear and embrace the spirit of revelation? What would it look like if the church in America would reject the spirit of control by division and embrace the spirit of power, love, and a sound mind?

Without vision, people cast off restraint, and if today it seems that our nations are struggling to cast off the last vestiges of restraint, it is because the people of God have lost their vision and have become barren. Let us stop looking to world leaders for vision and provision. The fruitfulness that we long for is grounded in the vision of Christ's body as faithful managers of the mysteries of God for the sake of the world. And perhaps, just perhaps, if the people of God were to embrace the vision of God, then maybe who gets elected to political office does not really matter as much as we think it does.

DREAMING

After this I will pour out My Spirit on all humanity;
then your sons and your daughters will prophesy,
your old men will have dreams, and your young
men will see visions.

Joel 2:28

You all know how it is. You read something over and over again throughout your whole life, and then suddenly the Holy Spirit breathes[11] on it causing it to take on a life of its own. I have been captivated by this message "your old men will have dreams" (literally, "dream dreams"). Here is the way I see the world. Visionaries and entrepreneurs have dreams. Young people have dreams. But then you get old, and in this world, old people don't have a dream; that's what makes them old.

There are four kinds of old in this country. There are the wealthy-, enfranchised-, empowered-old that have "made it" and just want to spend their latter years in leisure. They have no dream. Then there are the not wealthy-, disenfranchised-, disempowered-old that have nothing to look forward to in their latter years but the same daily grind by which they have survived all the long, weary years of life. They have no dream. Then there are the in-betweeners, the enfranchised, and empowered, but not necessarily wealthy, who are striving in the hope of "making it" so that they can have some leisure in their latter years. At best, they have a vain dream.

There was a time back when I was in the Air Force, when the average life span for people retiring from the military was 3½ years post-retirement. Part of this was lifestyle, but part of it was simply the loss of purpose and identity. Without a vision, without a dream, people perish.

I have a friend, now in glory, upon whom the Spirit was clearly poured out. In the year or so before he retired, he discovered again what it means to be a dearly beloved child of God, and he began to dream. My friend retired with the dream of starting a youth center in our town so that kids would have a place to go after school. He died from a brain tumor before he saw his dream, but it didn't matter; he had a dream. You know what I mean by "it didn't matter"? Have you been around someone who had a dream? It's what they live for. It becomes part of their identity. It empowers them, fills them with hope and purpose and abundant life. They live present-future. They are always striving to stand on the thin edge between the now and the not yet, but their world just keeps growing until one day, they finally do hit that boundary, and without a single regret or hesitation, they step over that line and into the heart of Father.

But without a dream, people feel like they are done—it's over. They feel like they've been benched, put out to pasture, put on the shelf; they are irrelevant, forgotten in some closet somewhere; they've outlived their usefulness. There is simply nothing left for them to do. Their world keeps shrinking and shrinking until it finally falls in upon them.

But that's the way of world. That is not life in the Spirit. God says:

> *When I pour out My Spirit, your old men will dream dreams.*

And so I found myself standing in front of my church on a Sunday morning declaring that God was pouring out His Spirit so that old men would once again have a dream. I believe that this passage spoken by my namesake, "Your old men will have dreams, and your young men will see visions," goes hand-in-hand with what God spoke through Malachi, "Look, I am going to send you Elijah . . . and he will turn the hearts of fathers to their children and the hearts of children to their fathers."[12]

What happens when fathers have no dream, or sons have no vision? You can see it all over this country. Many of our cities appear to have already been struck by the desolating curse of fatherlessness. Fathers don't stop being fathers because they don't love their children, but because they themselves have no dream, no hope, no purpose, no sense of a future toward which, and from which, they are living. And when they look at their sons, they see no vision, no hope of legacy. Without a dream there is no hope of living present-future, and old men cease to be fathers; they can only live past-present, trapped in the memories of what was, or in the moment of what is. Children don't cease honoring their fathers because they don't love them, but because either they have a vision and cannot respect a man with no dream, or because they lack vision and have no use for an old man who can give them no hope of any kind of legacy.

But dreams are contagious and vision is invigorating.

When the Spirit of God is poured out and old men begin to dream dreams and young men have vision, everything changes. When a young man without vision finds himself loved by an old man with a dream, he will call that man father. He will serve him until that old man's dream takes root in his own heart and springs up into vision. When an old man without a dream is honored by a young man with vision, he will call him son, and he will be strengthened by the vision of the young until a new dream is awakened in him. So the hearts of fathers will be turned to the children because a new dream will be kindled in them by the outpouring of the Spirit. The hearts of the children will be turned to the fathers because a new vision will rise up within them by the outpouring of the Spirit. And when the hearts beating with passion for an unfulfilled dream are bound together with hearts energized by a vision of the future, then a voice will be heard again in the wastelands of our cities:

> *Behold, I will do a new thing, Now it shall spring forth; shall you not know it? I will even make a road in the wilderness and rivers in the desert.*

> Isaiah 43:19, NKJV

So, where do you find yourself today? Are you an old man without a dream or a young man lacking vision? I write this specifically to you fathers. As surely as I breathe, this is the word of the Lord for you today. Jesus said that Elijah has already come, and we know that the Spirit has already been poured out, so this is happening now. This is not for some day or one day; this is for today. It is time to set everything else aside, to break up the fallow ground of your heart and to seek the Lord until He comes and rains righteousness on you.

When the dreams begin to grow, don't dismiss them; nurture them.

This is God's heart for you, and for this world.

LOST?

Few things are more critical when facing adversity than getting our minds right. Many believers live from earth to heaven more focused on their problem than on the grace of God that could be manifest in their situations. We try to encourage people by telling them to "keep looking up" when what we really need is a complete change in perspective. We should not be telling people to keep looking up but to keep looking down. Paul writes in Ephesians 2:

> *And God has raised us up with Christ and seated us with Him in the heavenly realms.*

v 6, NIV

We should be living now from heaven to earth with a focus on the grace of God that is there for us to walk out the good works God has prepared for us in advance. Where we see adversity, God sees opportunity. Where we see problems, God sees potential. Where we see wrecks, God sees works. We have been saved by grace so that God could display in us His kindness and His immeasurable grace, but we have to get our minds right. We have to get God's perspective, and for this we need the mind of Christ.

Paul also writes in 1 Corinthians 2 that there is a wisdom God has predestined for our glory. It is wisdom that was hidden in mystery that has now been revealed to us by the Spirit of God. He goes on to write that "we have the mind of Christ" (v. 16). That is amazing. I have the mind of Christ. You have the mind of Christ. The problem is we don't know how to access Christ's mind because His thoughts are so different from ours. It is like being lost and having a GPS navigator in our hands for which we do not know the password. Our perspective is skewed because we can only see where we are now and we do not know where that is. We are stuck looking up for help to satellites we cannot see. We know they are there, but we cannot access them. If we just had the password for the GPS, then instantly our perspective would change. Suddenly we would be looking down on our location from above rather than looking up from below. We would be able to see the big picture, and we would no longer be lost, even if we had not yet moved from our current location. Lost is a state of mind, not a geographical location. If we could access the GPS, we would know where we were and where we are going. Fear would be displaced by purpose and while there may still be a journey ahead of us, there would be joy for the journey. This is what it means to have a renewed mind, to have our perspective shifted, so that we are seeing from heaven to earth.

So how do we access the mind of Christ?

Those who know me for any length of time know that I believe gratitude and repentance are the master keys to the Kingdom of God. Gratitude and repentance are good places to start. The shift in focus begins with gratitude and becomes an act of repentance, changing the way we think.

But there is a specific step we need to take in order to access the mind of Christ—a password if you will. Paul gives us the password in Philippians 2:5:

Let this mind be in you . . .[13]

The attitude of Christ is the key to accessing the mind of Christ.

One of the first things that adversity does is to strike at our own self-centeredness. Adversity strikes at the way we feel things ought to be.

"This isn't right!"

"This isn't fair!"

"I deserve to be treated better than this!"

"This is not how it is supposed to be!"—etc., etc., ad nauseam. As long as our thoughts stay earthbound, we may have the mind of Christ, but His mind/His thoughts will be as inaccessible to us as a GPS or a computer for which we lack the password. Accessing the mind of Christ begins simply by having the same attitude as Christ, who "while existing in the form of God, did not consider equality with God as something to be used for his own advantage."[14]

Let that soak in for a moment. Christ knew exactly who He was. He existed in the form of God; He was equal with God yet refused to use His equality with God for His own advantage. Humility is the password to accessing the mind of Christ. I'm not referring to the religious humility—that which leads you to believe you are merely a lowly sinner saved by grace and, therefore, just need to surrender to whatever comes your way as though it were God's will. There is a true humility in which a son or daughter of God knows that he or she is a joint heir of Christ who is seated with Him in heavenly places, yet is willing to lay aside all earthbound thoughts of rights, reputation, position, or entitlement, even to the point of death to self. That is the humility that gives us access to the mind of Christ. The moment we let go of our own thoughts, we become open to His. The moment we stop being concerned about our rights and our reputation, we open ourselves to the hidden wisdom of God.

Are you facing adversity right now? Where do you feel it striking? You need to access the mind of Christ, and for that you need the humility of Christ. When you learn to "Let this mind be in you," then your entire perspective will shift. You will see the grace of God, and experience the immeasurable kindness of God towards you in Christ. The Spirit who searches the depths of God will reveal to you all that has been freely given to you by God.

Whatever your current crisis, walking through it full of grace and truth while maintaining a heaven-to-earth perspective is precisely the good work that God has prepared for you to walk in.

PROMISE

For I am not ashamed of the gospel . . . For in it God's righteousness is revealed from faith to faith, just as it is written: The righteous will live by faith.

Romans 1:16, 17

Now without faith it is impossible to please God.

Hebrews 11:6

For the land you are entering to possess is not like the land of Egypt, from which you have come, where you sowed your seed and irrigated by hand as in a vegetable garden. But the land you are entering to possess is a land of mountains and valleys, watered by rain from the sky. It is a land the LORD your God cares for. He is always watching over it from the beginning to the end of the year.

Deuteronomy 11:10-12, HCSB

I t would appear on the surface that nothing connects the first two verses above with the third, but I have stumbled onto the connection via a book by Gary Burge[15] and it is challenging. Let me review quickly how I think about faith. Faith does not belong to the realm of the known, the certain, the actual (what is); but faith belongs to the realm of the unknown, the uncertain, the possible (what could be). The realm of the unknown is the realm where in this world doubt, uncertainty, dissatisfaction, and anxiety are manifest. It is to this place that faith belongs. This means that as long as we insist on living in the realm of the known, certain, and the actual—where faith is not required—we cannot please God.

Now consider this phrase: God's righteousness is revealed from faith to faith.[16] The righteousness of God is not revealed in the realm of the known, certain, and actual. The righteousness of God is revealed from the place of faith, the place of the unknown, uncertain, and possible. Furthermore, the righteousness of God is not revealed to bring us from the unknown and uncertain to a place of the known and certain, but to bring us from faith to faith. In other words, the revelation of the rightness of who God is and what He is doing brings us from the place of the unknown and the uncertain where faith is required to live, to another place of the unknown and the uncertain where faith is required to live. Why would God do any less? If it is impossible to please God without faith, then why would a good and loving God put us in a place where we can live without faith?

So what does this have to do with "the land you are entering to possess"? We tend to romanticize the idea of the Promised Land. This was a land of promise (the possible), not a land of certainty. That is the point Moses is making. The people are going to have to dramatically change the way they live in order to enter this land. Entering the land of promise requires a paradigm shift. Israel's time in the wilderness, living by daily faith in the miraculous provision of God, was designed to break them out of one way of living and to deliver them into a completely different way of living.

Here's the thing about the land of promise, the geography and the geology of the land itself required the people of Israel to live by faith. We think of "the Promised Land" as the place where blessing, certainty, and satisfaction come together, but in fact, the land of promise is the place where faith is continually tested. The land of promise was a land which required the people to live by constant faith in God to sustain them, defend them, and to define their lives.[17]

As Dr. Burge explains, in Egypt and Mesopotamia where the great civilizations arose, the land was relatively flat and lay along rivers, which enabled crops to be watered through irrigation canals. Inhabitants were not dependent upon rainfall for healthy crops but could plant anything they wanted because they could always engineer their own solutions. Not so in the land of promise. There is only one river, the Jordan, and the surrounding countryside is so hilly that it is impossible to use the Jordan to irrigate. Upon entering the land of promise, the people of Israel became absolutely dependent upon the two seasons of rainfall which God alone could give. They could only plant and harvest crops which flourished in those limiting conditions. The land of promise could only be watered by rain, thus the land of promise required that the people who lived there live by faith in the God who could make not only rain, but bread itself fall from heaven. Do you see it? God moved the Israelites from one place of uncertainty ("Will there be manna tomorrow morning?") to a place of greater uncertainty ("Will there be rain in three months so my barley will ripen?"), because the righteousness of God is revealed from faith to faith so that the righteous will live by faith.

Moreover, the geography of Israel is such that, unlike Egypt and Mesopotamia, it has no naturally defensible borders. In time of peace, the land was a highway for caravans between Egypt and Mesopotamia. In time of war, it was a highway for armies. There were no mountain passes, river fords, or deserts they could fortify against invaders. They could be invaded from North or South at any time. So Israel had to live by faith that God Himself would defend the land of promise because they could not.

Finally, this Promised Land was a place where Israel's identity as the people of God was constantly challenged by a flood of cultural and religious diversity. Israel entered a land that was already occupied by dozens of other cultures, and was soon to possess a land that would be flooded every caravan season with dozens of other cultures.

Now, let's think again about what it means to live in the land of promise. The land of promise is the place where:

> 1) You cannot engineer your own circumstances to bring yourself to a place of economic security but will always have to continuously trust God to sustain you.
>
> 2) You will always be open to attack from any direction at any time and will have to continually trust God to defend you.
>
> 3) You will be continually challenged by the religious and cultural plurality that surrounds you so that you will have to trust in God to define you.

So where is the Good News? This definition of the Promised Land just sounds hard, risky, and so uncertain. Well, to sum it all up, I think the Good News is simply that God has brought us out of a place where we cannot please Him into a place where we can. We have been brought from non-faith to faith, and now live from faith to faith.

The land of promise is a place of uncertainty, yes, but is also the place of promise. It is the place where God is revealing Himself; it is the place where He is rewarding those who earnestly seek Him; it is the place we need to be.

ANSWERS

*The answer is out there, Neo, It's looking for you.
And it will find you if you want it to.*

Morpheus from "The Matrix"

*Then the word of the LORD came to him: "Get up,
go to Zarephath that belongs to Sidon and stay
there. Look, I have commanded a woman who is a
widow to provide for you there."*

1 Kings 17:8

Where do we find our provision, our place, our miracle, our ministry? Where do we find our answers? I am fascinated by the idea that what we are looking for may be "out there" rather than "in here." Sometimes we press in to the church—to people we know, to Bible study, to prayer—and find . . . nothing. What if the answer is not to be found in pressing in but in going out? What if God were as much "out there" as He is "in here"? What if "pressing in to God" does not mean another prayer meeting, another church service, or another conference, but simply means stepping out to a new and unfamiliar place in search of a widow with a word?

Elijah was the father of Israel's prophets, yet there came a day when there was nothing for him in Israel. Instead, God sent him out to a foreign land in search of a widow with a word. That was really radical. Even in Jesus' day, Israel had not yet learned that Israel's God had more on His heart than just Israel. This was a vital lesson in Elijah's day, and it is a vital lesson today: God is just as active and just as engaged "out there" as "in here." In order to find his place, his provision, his miracle, his ministry, Elijah had to go out from Israel, Israel's customs and Israel's religious values, and enter into a relationship with a non-believer in a foreign land. How paradigm shifting is that? The father of Israel's prophets finds his provision, his place, his miracle, his ministry in a relationship with a non-believer.

God's word to Elijah was simply a command to get up and go. There was no miraculous power in that word; it was a word of positioning rather than a word of empowering. It was a word designed simply to get Elijah out of his current circumstance and into the place where there was already a word of power waiting to be released. The power and the miracle were in the word that had already been spoken over someone else in some other place—but Elijah had to go out and find it.

When Elijah found his widow, she was in the final moments of a meaningless life. She was preparing to die, completely unaware that a word of life was hanging over her. That's what we need to see here. God had already commanded the miracle, but the power of that word was not released until Elijah went out in search of it, found it, and activated it. What if the empowering word we are seeking is not to be found in the church but is "out there" already waiting for us to find it? What if while we sit "in here" waiting for God to move us, someone "out there" is dying for us to release the power of a word already spoken over them? Why would this be so?

We were created to be persons in relationship. If you are like me—an introvert raised in a society of individuals—then you would probably prefer to sit by a little stream and wait on God to bless you and provide for you directly.[18] That's okay for a season. But God never intended us to have a religion of "just me and God." God let Elijah sit by himself for a season, but for Elijah to continue to experience God's blessing, he had to step out into the unknown of a new relationship. The greater blessings of God come through relationships with others and those others are not always "in here." Sometimes the word of the Lord is not for "me" but for "we." Consequently, in order to release the power of that word, "me" has to get up and go out in search of the "we."

Abraham's children have a responsibility to live from the power of Abraham's blessing:

> *I will bless those who bless you . . . and all the*
> *peoples on earth will be blessed through you.*
>
> Genesis 12:3, HCSB

The issue here is that the prophetic word was not for Elijah's life alone but also for this foreign widow in a foreign land. She was not of Israel, and she did not acknowledge God as her God, yet God loved her and wanted to bless her. So God spoke a prophetic word of miraculous provision over her and her household, but it was a word that was without effect because she had no faith to connect to it and thus no way to activate it. She needed a son or daughter of Abraham, "the father of all those having faith," to connect with her in order to release the power of the word that had already been spoken over her.

We were not created for the mundane, but for the mystical. We are meant to be a people who by faith are pursuing the things of the Spirit of God. We know we are supposed to be living our lives "out there," but it is so much easier to turn in than to go out. And so sometimes we sit and wait on God hoping to be overwhelmed by the Holy Spirit or overtaken by a miracle, because sometimes what we really want is fearlessness without faith, power without process, or results without risk. But that's not mystical: that's magical, and God doesn't do magic. So, sometimes God puts what we need "out there" in the hands of a foreigner and sends us out to find it.

Some words position us. Some words empower us. We must not confuse the two. I wonder if many of the prophetic words we receive "in here" are positioning words meant simply to get us "out there." Maybe it's time we take stock of ourselves and reconsider what God has spoken over us. If what God has spoken over us are positioning words, then it makes no sense for us to wait on God in order to be resourced and empowered before we get up and go. We just need to get up and go and trust that somewhere "out there" is a widow with a word who is just waiting for a son or daughter of Abraham to release the power of that word.

May I encourage you today that if you are still trying to find your provision, your place, your miracle, your ministry, the answer is out there. It's looking for you. And it will find you if you want it to. Go and find your widow.

DISAPPOINTMENT

How many of you have had the experience of being defined by someone else's disappointment? It can be a soul-crushing experience. Nothing good ever grows in the shadow of disappointment. The good news of the gospel is that we do not live in the shadow of God's disappointment but in the light of His love. Love bears all things, hopes all things, and believes all things.[19] Because God is love[20] He treats us according to His grace and His hope for our future in Christ. But this chapter is not about that. Our focus here is on how we define God by our disappointments.

Learning to live in a lifestyle of repentance means constantly evaluating **why** I am thinking and believing **what** I am thinking and believing. My current target of repentance is to discover how much I have defined God, myself, and others, by disappointment.

A few months ago, I was teaching a class, when we got onto the topic of healing and miracles. I simply asked the students if we could dare to dream together of building a place where the lame walked, the deaf heard, and the blind gained their sight. The response was not particularly positive. It became evident to me that night that together we were guilty of defining God by our disappointments. As I went around and talked to people individually, I was amazed by some of the stories I heard. Many of the people there had experienced or participated in some sort of miracle of healing. Yet it was not the miracles that were defining people's beliefs and expectations, but their disappointments. The response as a group was not "Yes, I have seen God heal, and I have experienced healing, so I believe God is Healer, and I want to pursue that." The response as a group was "I prayed for this person, and they are still sick," or "I prayed for this person, and they died. Therefore, I do not want to pursue this." It was not God's activity that was informing our belief systems but His apparent lack of activity. That is deity defined by disappointment. As I continue to think about this, I realize how much of a mirror they held up to me that night; I am guilty of defining God by my disappointments.

We struggle with a logical fallacy, which concludes that because not everyone is healed, God does not want to heal everyone. I would argue that this is a very specific example of us defining God by our disappointments. Would you conclude that because not everyone is saved, God does not want to save everyone? None but a strict Calvinist would make such a statement. Your response may be that I am talking apples and oranges here. However, in the entirety of the New Testament, there is only one dominating word in the Greek language which is used to indicate both salvation of the soul, and healing of the body—*sozo*. So literally, it is apples to apples. To say that not everyone is healed, therefore, God does not want to heal everyone is a complete non-sequitur; the first statement simply does not prove the second. At a minimum, when we believe this way, we are guilty of arguing the nature of God on the basis of human experience rather than on the basis of his self-revelation. That is a very dangerous thing to do. In fact, that was the basis for the original sin.[21]

If we set our own disappointments aside for just a moment and allow God to define Himself apart from our experience of Him, what do we find? What I see is that the first time God makes an "I AM" statement in the Bible, in other words, the first time He formally introduces Himself by name, it is to identify Himself as Healer—"I am the LORD who heals you."[22] If His eternal, unspeakably holy name is Healer, how can we say that He does not want to heal everyone? To make that statement is to claim that God is not living according to His own nature. In effect, we are accusing God of falling short of His own glory. We are saying to him, "Your name is one thing, but You are another." Then Jesus comes to make visible the invisible God. In Jesus the fullness of God's nature dwelt in bodily form. How was the fullness of that divine nature expressed in the flesh? Jesus healed all who came to Him. So if God defines Himself by word and deed as Healer, how can we say that He does not want to heal everyone? Only by defining God according to our own disappointments.

Please understand that this is not academic for me. I have prayed for many people—not lightly, not casually, not a "formal wish" tossed up without expectation. Some have been healed; some have not, some, including a man who loved me like his own son, died. So now I have to choose whether or not I will allow my disappointments to define God or whether I will allow God to define Himself.

We all have disappointments. Living productively with those disappointments is part of the price of believing. However, when I define deity by disappointment, I deface God and de-faith myself. You may feel that God is not (or was not) there for you, or that God is not meeting your needs, or that God does not want to heal you, or, or, or. . . . But hear me, beloved, it is a dangerous thing to keep God in the shadow of your own disappointments. Without faith it is **impossible** to please God, yet it takes no faith at all to believe that God does not want to do something that we do not see Him doing. Let me say that again a different way. If I do not see God healing everyone, it takes no faith at all for me to say that He does not want to heal everyone. That is a simple, human conclusion drawn from human experience.

May I encourage you today by the grace of God, to begin to consider with me the possibility that there are areas of our lives where we have defined God by disappointment? Without faith it is impossible to please God. With faith—any faith, no matter how small—pleasing God is just not that difficult.

BELIEVING

Love believes all things. God is love, therefore, God believes. What does God believe in? Whatever it is, God believed in it so much that He paid the price of believing.

The old hymn says, "Jesus paid it all . . ." Did He? The answer, of course, is yes, but does "Jesus paid it all" mean that there is no longer a price for us to pay? And the answer is . . . well, honestly, this is where a lot of Christians in this country start to stutter.

Those of us who live in America find it easy to embrace a price-less faith. How many of us have been hunted by our families? How many of us have lost jobs, homes, limb, or life because of a conviction that "Jesus paid it all"? I fear it is all too easy in our current social setting to sing the first part of that line and forget the rest: "Jesus paid it all, all to Him I owe." Where no one is waiting to exact the price of believing from us upon our declaration of faith, it is left to us to decide how much of that price we are willing to pay and when we will pay it. As a result, many of us live a price-less faith as if the song said, "Jesus paid it all" (period, full stop, end of line).

I have been wondering if perhaps most Christians in America could be categorized as being mystical, magical, or mundane. At one level these are world-view descriptions, but one of the common denominators has to do with the price of believing.

Christian mystics understand that the material is less significant than the spiritual. They live their lives in pursuit of a present spiritual reality. The theme song of the mystic could be—

> Holy Spirit ,You are welcome here,
> Come flood this place and fill the atmosphere
> Your glory, God, is what our hearts long for
> To be overcome by Your presence, Lord[23]

Mystics understand "Jesus paid it all" to mean that Jesus opened "a new and living way"[24] to a new life in God, but that there is still a price to be paid in exploring the new life that has been set before us. The mystic is not waiting for eternal life to begin; today is the day. A mystic believes that there is always more and that we are called to pursue that more in Christ,[25] because God has prepared something for us that is beyond our ability to ask, imagine, or even dream,[26] and the only limitations on a life of faith are the goodness of God and the price we are willing to pay to in pursuit of His will, "on earth as it is in heaven."

Mundane Christians are more convinced of the material than the spiritual. They live their lives in pursuit of a present material reality trusting that "someday" will take care of itself because "Jesus paid it all," thus today, there is no price to be paid and no pursuit to be made. The theme song of the mundane could be—

> Some glad morning when this life is o'er,
> I'll fly away;
> To a home on God's celestial shore,
> I'll fly away.[27]

If you find this description offensive, I'm sorry. My confession is that most of my Christian life has been mundane. The choice between the mystical and the mundane is sometimes a daily struggle for me. Some people (like me on some days) are mundane by choice, but I think most people are mundane through simple ignorance; our social setting is dominatingly mundane, and many of our churches have embraced mundane theology.

Some Christians are given to magical thinking. This is a tricky category. Like mystics, magicals understand that the material is less significant than the spiritual. The fundamental difference between the two is that magicals do not like mystery, while mystics embrace mystery. Part of the price of believing is the embrace of mystery; the reality that there are things happening beyond our control, beyond our understanding, and beyond our ability to understand. Magicals want spiritual power, but are unwilling to pay the price of believing. While mystics are willing to surrender to mystery, magicals will do everything in their power to reduce mystery to a manageable level. They seek for strong causal links between their actions, words, or thoughts, and a particular effect. They are driven by a need to understand, to define, and to predict outcomes based on behaviors. They want to be able to control spiritual forces based on formula, method, and training. Magicals often claim a word of faith, but in their pursuit of formulaic certainty and spiritual quid pro quo, they end up rejecting mystery and denying faith.

As I alluded to in the chapter titled "Disappointment," a lot of this crystallized for me when I was in a discussion about divine healing. I have come to the realization that one of the reasons we end up defining God by disappointment is that the act of believing requires us to walk in mystery, and walking in mystery is costly. The mystic can believe that God wants to heal everyone, and is willing to pay the price that mystery demands when not everyone is healed and there are no answers as to why. The magical is unwilling to pay that price, and so "God wants to heal everyone" can become "God will heal everyone where there is right faith/action." The mundane, being essentially a dualist, simply refuses to pursue the subject because God is sovereign, and what matters is not this life, but the next.

I am reminded again of my roots. I grew up in mostly Assemblies of God churches, where one of the four cardinal doctrines is that divine healing is an integral part of the gospel. Deliverance from sickness is provided for in the atonement, and is the privilege of all believers. We said we believed it, but we did not act like we believed it.

Let me pose a question. If atonement was for all, and divine healing was provided for in the atonement, does that not mean that divine healing is for all? What does "Jesus paid it all" mean in this context? Will we continue to define deity by our disappointment resulting in the insistence that all of the atonement is for all, but part of the atonement is only for some?

If God is Healer by name and by nature, and divine healing is the privilege of all believers, then why are we not pursuing this at every opportunity? I think the bottom line answer is that some days we are unwilling to pay the price of believing. We are unwilling to pay the price of preparing ourselves for the works God has prepared for us. We are unwilling to pay the price of inconveniencing ourselves to "stop for the one" as Heidi Baker, a missionary to Mozambique, would say. We are unwilling to pay the price of our own reputations if we pray for someone and nothing appears to happen in that moment. We are unwilling to pay the price of sorrow to carry in our memory the faces and pain of the people for whom we have prayed who are still disabled or are still suffering (as if Jesus were not a man of sorrow). There is a price to believing. Where I am willing to pay the price, I believe. Where I am not willing to pay the price, I do not believe. I propose it is that simple.

Who and what are you "believing" for: salvation, healing, deliverance, freedom, destiny, legacy? Jesus paid it all, but there is a still a price to be paid—even in this country where no one waits with rope, knife, or fire to exact that price from us. Real faith is costly. Believing without seeing is costly. Embracing mystery is costly. Pursuing the things of God is costly. Is our faith priceless or price-less?

God believed, and Jesus paid the price of His believing. Will the Lamb of God receive the reward of His suffering? Perhaps, but only if we, too, are willing to pay the price of believing.

HAPPINESS

I had a bit of a revelation today—a bit of a change in thinking—and it's still messing with my head. Basically, I happened into an area where a lot of us may think we are being mystical when we are really just being mundane.

I have seen this quote from Max Lucado bouncing around for a while:

God's goal is not to make you happy. It is to make you His.

It has always bothered me, but until now, I have not been able to figure out why. Now this is going to get really messy, so please hear me out before reacting. I think Lucado's statement does not adequately account for generational and cultural differences in how we hear and think. Lucado fails to understand that while a good, rational Christian modernist can automatically assume all of the same things Lucado is assuming, any postmodernist is going to simply parse his statement at face value. When you do that, you can see that while his statement includes a great truth—God wants to make you His—it also includes a great untruth—

God's goal is not to make you happy. That's what I want to focus on because for many of us, religion too easily reduces Lucado's statement to "God doesn't want you happy." So today I find it is time to rethink the question, "What is wrong with happiness?"

Like most well-schooled religious thinkers, I have understood that happiness, by definition, is dependent upon circumstances, i.e., happiness depends upon what is happening. So then, happiness is circumstantial, and transient, and thus belongs to the realm of the mundane. We, well-intentioned religious people, understand that what is really important is not happiness, but joy.

The problem here is that, for the nonreligious person, joy is hard to define, and even harder to experience aside from happiness. How does one define joy without happiness? What does joy look like? If you see it, how do you know what you are seeing? Have you ever seen someone looking sad, anxious, depressed, angry, and said to yourself, "Now that right there is a person of joy"? No, of course not. So how do we know someone has joy? Is it not because they look, act, and (seem to) feel happy? When we see someone acting happy when happenings are good, we say they are happy. But when we see someone acting happy when happenings are bad, then that person has joy (or they are crazy, but let's not go there for this discussion). But then are we not guilty of defining joy based on circumstances? Being happy in good happenings is happiness, but looking or acting happy in bad happenings must be joy?

But what if we have it all wrong? What if Lucado's statement is like software that comes pre-bundled with religious malware? Nowhere do I see the Bible pitting our happiness and God's possession of us against each other as if they must be in opposition to each other or one must be favored over the other. At face value, Lucado pits God's interests against our happiness.

But what does the Bible say? Psalm 144:15 is explicit:

Happy are the people whose God is the Lord.

Lucado says, "God's goal is not to make you happy, but to make you His." But the Bible says that when we are His, the result is that we are happy. Ergo, God's goal is to make us happy, because God does not separate being happy from being His as we do.

You may argue that the word used here in Psalm 144:15, *ashrei*, does not really mean "happy", because you will see various English translations flip-flop between "happy" (*ashrei*) and "blessed" (*baruch*). But if you really look at the original language, one sees that in either Hebrew or in Aramaic, the word is completely interchangeable as happy or blessed, and has to do specifically with what is "happening." The good old King James Version translates the word 27 times as "blessed" and 18 times as "happy," but each time refers to circumstances that derive from being in relationship with God. Because what is happening in relation to God is good, one is (or should be) happy. The Old Testament ideal of the *shalom* of God was the rule of God manifested in a way that resulted in everyone's happiness. God is ours, and we are His; so happiness happens because all happenings are God's, and we are His. So, should the New Testament revelations of our position and possession in Christ take us forward from this ideal of happiness . . . or should they take us somewhere else?

Perhaps we have been caught up in a subtle, but powerfully dualistic delusion. We believe that joy is spiritual, while happiness is material (I did, until about three hours before writing this). Joy is eternal, while happiness is transient. Joy is mystical, while happiness is mundane. But this is the trap. We think we are being mystical by saying that joy has more value or is of greater importance than happiness, but the reality is that we are simply being mundane. Yes, happiness is circumstantial, but the way we think of joy as "greater than" and happiness as "less than" forces our minds into considering our circumstances in mundane ways rather than in mystical ways. Why? Because happiness is a mystical not a mundane quality. Why? Because happiness is dependent upon what is happening, but it is time to rethink what is really happening. I affirm that happiness is purely circumstantial, but if I strive for mystical rather than mundane thinking, then my circumstances are dominated by the mystical rather than the mundane. My circumstances are not rooted on earth, but in heaven. So what is happening that could/should define my happiness?

> **• I have been given the right to be called a child of God.** Shouldn't that make me happy?

> **• I can walk as a brother and joint heir of Christ.** Shouldn't that make me happy?

> **• I have been seated in heavenly places with Christ.** Shouldn't that make me happy?

> **• God is working out everything for my good**. Shouldn't that make me happy?

I could go on, but you get the idea.

You could argue that what I am illustrating is joy not happiness. If that is what you are thinking, then you are missing the point. Happiness is circumstantial; it is by definition dependent upon what is happening. The challenge here is to stop being mundane in our thinking about what is happening. A mystic focuses on what is "happening" in heavenly places rather than what is "happening" on earth, thus happiness happens in Christ. What is happening right now, whenever and wherever "right now" may be, is that the Holy Spirit is in you and in me telling us that we are His—a child of God. Shouldn't this happening result in happiness? What is happening right now is that the Holy Spirit is filling my heart with Father's love. Shouldn't this happening result in happiness? Again, I could go on.

The point is that it is only a mundane kind of thinking that makes happiness a "less than" and joy a "more than." Yes, happiness is dependent upon circumstances, but only mundane thinking believes that our circumstances are anything less than happy and blessed in Christ Jesus. It is only a mundane dualism that keeps our focus on the circumstances of the material world and blinds us to what is happening in heavenly places. So while religion wants to deny the role of happiness in life, and philosophy wants us to believe that there is more to life than the pursuit of happiness, I am thinking maybe they are both wrong. For the mystic, perhaps, the pursuit of happiness—the pursuit of our position and our possession—that has happened, is happening, and will happen in Christ is **all** there is to this life.

Consider what Frances Crosby says has happened, is happening, and will happen:

> Blessed assurance, Jesus is mine!
> O what a foretaste of glory divine!
> Heir of salvation, purchase of God,
> Born of His Spirit, washed in His blood.
> Perfect submission, perfect delight!
> Visions of rapture now burst on my sight;
> Angels descending bring from above
> Echoes of mercy, whispers of love.
> Perfect submission, all is at rest!
> I in my Savior am happy and blessed,
> Watching and waiting, looking above,
> Filled with His goodness, lost in His love.[28]

If this is **our** story, and this is **our** song, shouldn't that make us happy?

MYSTERY

A person should consider us in this way: as servants
of Christ and managers of God's mysteries. In this
regard, it is expected of managers that each one of
them be found faithful.

1 Corinthians 4:1-2

have been fascinated for a few months now by Paul's idea of
being "managers of God's mysteries." I think a lot of people in
church understand what it means to be "servants of Christ," but
"managers of mysteries"? Allow me to take a moment to break
down a couple of the words and then build back to what I think
is a really important idea.

First let's look at "mysteries" from which we derive the idea
of a "mystic," meaning one who is connected with, or initiated
into, mysteries. A *mysterion*, or "mystery", is something that
is intended to be both hidden and revealed—hidden from the
mundane or casual seeker, but revealed to those who diligently
seek for it. Paul writes in 1 Corinthians 14:2 that one who speaks

in spiritual language is speaking "mysteries in the Spirit." In 1 Corinthians 2, Paul writes of "hidden wisdom in a mystery" that is beyond our natural ability to apprehend or comprehend but which has been revealed to us by the Spirit of God. Paul goes on to distinguish human wisdom from spiritual things which can only be understood by spiritual people. My first point here is that when we see "mysteries" in the Bible, this should excite us. The hidden things of God are not hidden because they are meant to stay hidden rather; they are hidden because they are meant to be sought after. Has anyone ever given an Easter egg hunt with the intent that the eggs not be found? So it is with the mysteries of God. Proverbs 25:2 says:

> *It is the glory of God to conceal a matter and the glory of kings to investigate a matter.*

Many years ago a person described to me a vision he'd had of me. I was on an Easter egg hunt with basket in hand joyfully "finding" one treasure-filled egg after another. While I thought I was "finding" all of these eggs, what I could not see were the angels who were moving along ahead of me, constantly laying down more eggs for me to "find," and—here is the punch line— just in front of them was a giant dump truck full of Easter eggs from which the angels were replenishing their stock. That's a vision for all of us! We can exhaust the mundane so quickly. I say, "exhaust" because the pursuit of the mundane is so very wearying. This consumer–driven, commercial world we live in as Americans exists to offer us the next big and exciting, yet totally mundane and ultimately unsatisfying thing; but the *mysterion* of God are inexhaustible—and that should make us as happy as children on an Easter egg hunt.

Next is the idea of "managers" or *oikonomous*. The word literally means, "household manager," but it is usually translated as "manager" or "steward". This is actually where we get our word "economy" from *oikonomia*, which means, "the rules of the house" (for good management). This may be a new thought for some of you but there is an economy to the mysteries of God. We are expected to be good managers of this economy. What does it mean to be a good manager? I think all good, humanly understood principles of management apply here, so feel free to explore this idea more on your own. Allow me to offer a couple of thoughts as well.

In Luke 16, Jesus distinguishes between unrighteous (mundane) wealth and genuine (mystical) riches. Hidden in this passage are two keys to God's economy:

> *Whoever is faithful in very little is also faithful in much, and whoever is unrighteous in very little is also unrighteous in much. So if you have not been faithful with the unrighteous money, who will trust you with what is genuine? And if you have not been faithful with what belongs to someone else, who will give you what is your own? No household slave can be the slave of two masters, since either he will hate one and love the other, or he will be devoted to one and despise the other. You can't be slaves to both God and money.*

> vs 10-13, HCSB

First, this passage suggests that God may test us in the mundane before entrusting us with the mystical. Second, but inseparable from the first, it is inferred that we have to choose which economy to devote ourselves to. What many people miss is that the harder test is not in lack, but in excess. The test of our faithfulness in the mundane (and thus our readiness for the mystical) is not what we do when do not have enough, but what we do when we have more than enough. One of the reasons we, in America, frequently live in mystical lack is that it is so easy for us to spend our mundane excess on satisfying our own desires.[29] This is the question: if we spend our mundane excess to please, promote, preserve, or empower ourselves, then how can God trust us with the mystical? Consider what would happen if God entrusted a gift of healing to someone who had proved themselves unfaithful in the mundane. Can we not imagine the damage that could be done by someone who used the true riches of heaven to please, promote, preserve, or empower themselves? The principle is that when we prove ourselves trustworthy in the economy of the mundane, we open ourselves up to an increase in the economy of mystery. [Now lest we descend into dualism here, in thinking that we have to completely separate ourselves from the mundane in order to pursue the mystical, let me add that Jesus tells us that if we seek first to live in the Kingdom (the economy of mystery), what we need in the economy of the mundane will be added to us.[30]]

Next, having chosen to live in the economy of mystery, we need to prove ourselves faithful in little before expecting much. Human wisdom can be possessed; God's wisdom, hidden in mystery, must be continuously pursued. Do we understand the difference between possessing and pursuing? The mysteries of God are like a good woman. A wise husband understands that the wedding ceremony does not mean the pursuit is over. The newly married man has not been given possession of a woman; rather, he has been given an exclusive license, and an open invitation, to pursue this one woman for the rest of his life. Mystery is possessed only so long as it is pursued.

Being faithful in the little things means that we gratefully accept little things from God and begin to use what He gives us even while seeking (not demanding) more. We could say that mysteries are like yarn. God never gives us the whole ball of yarn at once, because we would just get all tangled up in it and make a giant mess of things. God is pleased, however, to put a bit of yarn in our hand. So long as we continue to pull on that single bit of yarn, wrapping it up as we go along, we can form our own ball of yarn which will continue to grow until we can begin to make things from that yarn, which we can give away to others. Being faithful in the little things means not despising small beginnings, but working consistently and gratefully with what we've been given while pursuing the possibility of more.

The last thought I want to offer is one that requires greater faith. This is often where we have to pay the price of believing. Managers of mystery have to commit to participating in and demonstrating things that are beyond comprehension or expression. As the old-timers used to say, "Some things are better caught than taught," or "Some things are better felt than telt." In other words, some things cannot be comprehended; they can still be apprehended, but first they have to be demonstrated. I can apprehend the incomprehensible love of God, not because it has been explained, but because it has been demonstrated.[31]

I can't explain speaking in tongues, but I can demonstrate it. I can't explain dreams, visions, and prophecy, but I can participate in them, and I am learning to demonstrate them. I do not understand and cannot explain why some people are healed and some people are not, but as a faithful manager of mystery, I refuse to define God by my disappointment, and I refuse to let discussion displace demonstration.

Paul was a brilliantly trained, brilliantly skilled orator who was conversant in both the wisdom of men and the wisdom of God, yet he made a choice in Corinth to be a faithful manager of God's mysteries. He said:

When I came to you, brothers, announcing the testimony of God to you, I did not come with brilliance of speech or wisdom. For I didn't think it was a good idea to know anything among you except Jesus Christ and Him crucified. I came to you in weakness, in fear, and in much trembling. My speech and my proclamation were not with persuasive words of wisdom but with a powerful demonstration by the Spirit so that your faith might not be based on men's wisdom but on God's power.

1 Corinthians 2:1-5

That is my challenge, and one I hope you will join me in. I want to be more than a servant of Christ; I want to be a faithful manager of His mysteries. That means choosing to live in the economy of mystery, valuing demonstration over discussion, and not despising small beginnings.

Let the hunt begin . . .

BETWEEN

When I was young, I thought Jesus came to the earth so He could die on a cross, so I could be forgiven of my sins, so when I died I could go to heaven. To me that was the gospel. This is what my friend Dano would call the "gospel of salvation." It is true; it is real; it is powerful. But it is also just too small a story to be living in. We have been living with this mini-gospel for so long that it has become normative. Evangelical and Reformed theologians alike despair from pulpit, book, and magazine over the continuous stream of polls from Barna and Gallup which demonstrate that evangelical Christians are as sexually immoral and self-serving as non-Christians. Evangelical Christians divorce, beat their spouses and children, sleep around, hate their neighbors of a different skin color, don't give to the poor, etc., just as much as non–Christians do. In fact, divorce may be more common among evangelical Christians than in the general American population, and 90% of divorced evangelicals got divorced after they became Christians. Why is this happening? I think it is because we are living in too small a story. The first century gospel turned the world upside down. The 20th century gospel in America is often just enough to save us in our dying, but it seems, it is not enough to save us in our living.

What if God is telling a bigger story than the gospel of salvation? What if the gospel is not just about sinners being saved so they can go to heaven when they die or be caught up in some rapture that will happen someday? What if the gospel of the Kingdom of God is about dead slaves becoming living sons right here, right now?

The gospel of the Kingdom is not just for "Someday;" it is for now. The gospel is not just the good news that you were a sinner who has been forgiven and is now in the process of being sanctified. We have made that gospel story too small, too individualistic, and too subjective. It has a form of godliness but it lacks the power to transform lives beyond each one's own little world.

There is a bigger story. There is a bigger gospel that says once upon a time you were dead in your trespasses and sin, but now you have been made alive in Christ with a life that should spill out of you like a river in the desert. Once upon a time you were a slave in the kingdom of darkness, but now you have been brought into the Kingdom of Jesus and been made a son, a brother, and a coheir; you are now the light of the world. Once you were alienated from God and from each other, but now you have been brought near to the one who is closer than a brother, and you have been given the power and authority to draw others near to Him as well. Once you were defiled by your sin but now you have been made clean so that you can live, breathe, and move in the majesty of God's holy presence. Once you were under a curse, but now you are blessed in order to be a blessing. Once you were crippled by shame so that you fell short of His glory, but now you are healed to live from glory to glory with ever increasing glory. Once you were lost and wandering, but now you are following the Shepherd and Guardian of your soul as He leads you along the path of life. Once you were empty and hopeless with your best efforts being futile and vain, but now you are full. You have been given purpose and destiny, and now even your failures can be redeemed.

This gospel is for Today, it is not for Someday when you die or Jesus comes to take you away. It is for such a time as this that you have come into your favored position. Maybe, just maybe, if we start giving people a gospel to live for rather than a gospel to die for, things will change.

Maybe it all comes down to this question: How are we defining the "now" and the "not yet" of the Kingdom of God? People came to Jesus and asked Him, "Is it now that You are going to establish Your Kingdom?"[32] What if His kingdom has already come? Jesus told Mary, "My time has not yet come."[33] Yet Mary, by faith turned "not yet" into "now." Can we, who are filled with the Holy Spirit, do any less? We were born for Now. Imagine that Jesus is actually living within us each day as we move past the sin-defiled, the shame-crippled, the alienated, the dead, the cursed, and the lost. Imagine that He is now asking us, "Is it now that you are going to establish My kingdom"? What if Jesus is the one saying, "Now, now, now is the time!" and we are the ones saying, "Not yet"? What does "Behold, the Kingdom of God is within you"[34] actually mean?

May we not be so caught up with the "Not yet" that we fail to seize the "Now."

BREATHE

What would it sound like if we could strip away a 2000-year-old layer of theological presuppositions and hear the Scriptures as they were written? English has changed a great deal since the first time someone attempted to translate the New Testament into English. Consider the Greek word *pneuma*, which means, "wind or breath" generally, and only by context means, "spirit." Words are just containers into which we put meaning. The container labeled "boot" and "bonnet" contain very different content depending upon whether one is reading *Little House On the Prairie* or listening to Dr. Who. We have a problem when the contents of a container are determined by context, because our context today is not just different, it is bigger, thicker, more massive in some ways, and dramatically less massive in others than the context in which the New Testament was written. Every English translation of the Bible has a few errors here or there because of the theological context of the translators. What if we try to disremember what we know and just read the text as written? Is it possible that the text could come alive again in a new way? Following is an attempt to do just that. Most is quoted directly from *The Unvarnished New*

Testament.[35] Again, take a breath; try to disremember; read with fresh eyes, and see where this takes you.

> *And the LORD God formed man [of] the dust of the ground, and **breathed** into his nostrils the **breath** of life; and man became a living soul.*[36]

> *And he was proclaiming, "I bathed you in water, but he will bathe you in holy **breath**."*[37]

> *And it happened in those days that Jesus came from Nazareth, Galilee, and was bathed in the Jordan by John. And coming straight out of the water he saw the skies split apart and the **breath** like a dove coming down upon him.*[38]

> *Answered Jesus, "Truly, truly I tell you: anyone who isn't born of water and breath can never get into the kingdom of God. What's born of the flesh is flesh, and what's born of the **breath** is **breath**. Don't be amazed because I told you you have to be born again. The wind blows where it will and you hear the sound of it, but you don't know where it comes from or where it goes; it's the same with everyone born of the **breath**."*[39]

> *Jesus, though, knowing inside that his students were grumbling about that, said to them: "Does that throw you? Then what if you see the son of humanity ascending where he was before? **Breath** is the lifegiver, flesh serves for nothing. The words I have said to you are **breath** and life.*[40]

*Here I am sending you out like sheep amid wolves, so be smart as snakes and innocent as doves. Be careful of the world, because they'll hand you over to the judges and flog you in their synagogues. You'll be hauled before governors and kings because of me, as a testimony to them and the pagans. But when they hand you over, don't worry how you'll talk or what you'll say: you will be given something to say at that time, because it isn't you talking, it's the **breath** of the Father talking through you.[41]*

*Jesus said to them again, "Peace to you! Just as the Father sent me, so I send you." And so saying, he **breathed** upon them, saying, "Receive the sacred **breath**."[42]*

*And suddenly down from the sky came the rush of a driving wind of violent force and filled the whole house where they were sitting, and there appeared to them separate tongues of what looked like fire, which alighted upon each one of them, and they were all filled with holy **breath**.[43]*

*And don't be always drunk on wine, which brings a loss of self-control, but be filled with the **breath**, speaking to each other in psalms and hymns and religious songs.[44]*

Well, now that you've had an opportunity to try this out on your own, I want to share the three thoughts that lead me to this particular set of verses.

1) The re-creation event

Now do you see the connection between "the LORD God formed man [of] the dust of the ground, and breathed into his nostrils the breath of life; and man became a living soul" and "he [Jesus] breathed upon them, saying, 'Receive the sacred breath'"?

Pentecostals and non-Pentecostals can toss the second verse back and forth in various discussions about the baptism of the Holy Spirit, but all such discussions thoroughly miss the point. Jesus' breathing on the disciples is a recapitulation of the creation event. Through the first Adam, death entered and reigned over all mankind. Through the second Adam, who is also the embodiment of the Creator, life now enters and reigns over all who are in Christ. So, as Paul writes, all in Christ are a new creation. Why? Because Jesus, as both second Adam and Creator, takes our sin-dead bodies and breathes His life back into us, taking us out of the dominion of the first Adam's death into the dominion of the second Adam's life.

We do not have life in and of ourselves, but the life we now live, we live by faith in Jesus, and it is His breath that animates our true selves.

2) All those who are led by the breath of God are sons of God.

Abbes Hildegard used to describe herself as a feather on the breath of God. Jesus said that the wind blows where it will and you hear the sound of it, but you don't know where it comes from or where it goes; it's the same with everyone born of the breath. If we are truly being led by the breath of God, there will be an air of the inexplicable in our lives. Being led by the breath of God means we have to give up a concrete sense of knowing where we're going. Being led by the breath of God sometimes means allowing ourselves to be carried along like a feather on the breath of God.

3) Being filled with holy breath is as easy as breathing.

I realized with this fresh reading that being filled with holy breath really is as easy as breathing. This is why Paul writes—

> *Be filled with the spirit, speaking to each other in psalms and hymns and spiritual songs.*

Ephesians 5:19, The Unvarnished NT

As long as we are breathing out psalms and hymns and spiritual songs to one another, when we breathe in, we are breathing in sacred breath. Sacred breath can only be used to encourage, exhort, edify, worship, honor, express faith, etc. Sacred breath cannot be used to condemn, demean, injure, or to express worry, doubt, fear, anxiety, unholy anger, etc. Any breath taken for any of these negative purposes cannot be the sacred breath, and so we can no longer be filled with the breath at that point.

Do you want to be filled with holy breath? Focus on what you are breathing out, and then what you are breathing in will take care of itself.

BINARY

We are a binary people: two eyes, two ears, two feet, two hands. How many times have you heard someone say, "I only have two hands"? That's our limitation. We have only two hands, so our default mode of thinking is "on the one hand or on the other hand." That's the binary solution set. It is our normal default state. Our language evolves and revolves around the binary solution set. Here are just a few examples:

- Right or Wrong
- On or Off
- Black or White
- Good or Bad
- This or That
- War or Peace
- Sink or Swim
- Open or Closed
- For or Against
- Fight or Flight
- Win or Lose

There are two sides to every story, and when we personalize these choices, it becomes "my way or the highway." When things are really tough, it's "damned if you do; damned if you don't." You may be thinking that I have simply described the natural order of things, but quantum physics tells us differently (quantum superposition is key here), and so does the gospel.

The good news of the gospel is that God operates outside of our binary solution sets. Divine wisdom confronts binary thinking and calls us to a renewed mind that can perceive and reason in a new way. I see this throughout the Bible, but let me give you just a few examples in the following chapters of God confronting our binary thinking in three different areas of our lives. Think about how in each case God subverts the binary and attempts to draw the listener into a different paradigm.

Taking Sides

Joshua was near Jericho and saw a man standing with a drawn sword. He asks the man a question, "Are You for us or for our enemies?"

God answers, "Neither . . ."[45]

The Pharisees bring a woman caught in adultery to Jesus and present Him with an implied question, "Should this woman be stoned, or should she be let go?"

God answers, "Neither . . ."[46]

In these first two examples, people are trying to line up a binary set of "my side/their side—which side are you on?" Jesus demonstrates that there are not two sides to the story, but three. God is His own side, and He calls for all parties to leave their own side and come to His. In Joshua's story, we see people from both sides drawn to God's (Joshua and Rahab), but the tragedy of the second story is that only the adulteress is drawn to Jesus' side.

Question Without Answers

Jesus' disciples saw a blind man, and they ask Jesus a binary question, "Who sinned, this man or his parents . . . ?"

Jesus' answer is, "Neither . . . "[47]

Pharisees come to test Jesus and ask a binary question, "Is it right to pay taxes to Caesar, or not?"

Jesus' answer can be reduced to one word—"Both," or perhaps, "Neither."[48]

In both examples, Jesus is trying to get people to see that there is not a "right" or "wrong" answer for the questions, because of the nature of the questions themselves. Jesus is trying to pull the listeners into a completely new way of thinking.

Problems Without Solutions

The disciples present Jesus with a binary problem—"Send the crowds away to get food or they will be hungry."[49] Once again, Jesus denies the binary set with a divine "Neither": the crowd will neither be sent away, nor will the people go hungry.

Do you see what I am getting at here? We are so easily bound by our binary thinking, yet Jesus is trying to set us free. The natural order says that on the one hand, the people can go and buy food for themselves, or on the other hand, they can stay and be hungry. But Jesus stands before His disciples and declares that there is a third hand—His.

So let me ask: Are you being forced to takes sides? Do you have questions without answers? Are you facing problems without solutions? The gospel has good news for those who are brave enough to look beyond the horizon of the binary. In Christ, we have the opportunity to step out of the boat into the stormy waters where the answer is not "sink or swim" but "walk" as Jesus' hand becomes "the gripping hand" that draws Peter into a new paradigm.[50] On the one hand, you may make it; on the other hand, you may not. Look for the gripping hand in your life, and whether you turn to the right or the left you will hear a voice saying, "This is the way; walk in it."[51]

But . . .

Do you enjoy watching the TV show, "Jeopardy!"[52] —you know, the one where Alex Trebek presents the answers, and contestants have to guess the correct question? What if life were like the game of "Jeopardy!"? What if God's answers were to the questions we should have been asking? Have you ever stopped to consider what a life looks like when God hears our simple prayers/questions, and instead answers the prayers/questions being offered on our behalf by the Son through the Spirit? What if God's answers were all about calling our questions into question and inviting us to go further up and further in with Him? What if God is standing beside us like Alex Trebek saying, "And the answer is, 'My grace is sufficient for you,'" and our task is to discover the question?

Let me start with a highly provocative statement. I believe I can make a substantive case for the idea that God does not say "no" to those who love Him and are called according to His purpose.

Consider what Paul says in 2 Corinthians 2:18-20:

> *As God is faithful, our message to you is not "Yes and no." For the Son of God, Jesus Christ, who was preached among you by us . . . did not become "Yes and no"; on the contrary, a final "Yes" has come in Him. For every one of God's promises is "Yes" in Him. Therefore, the "Amen" is also spoken through Him by us for God's glory.*

Paul says that all of God's promises are "yes" in Jesus. In Christ, we are invited to live in a divine "yes" for the sake of His glory, a glory which He longs to share with us.[53] What I see in the Bible over and over again is the denial of the human insistence on a binary solution set (yes/no) and an attempt to cause us to reconsider the question.

In 2 Corinthians 12, we have a record of some man who saw things that were unseeable and heard things that were unspeakable. Because of these "extraordinary revelations" Paul writes:

> *So that I would not exalt myself, a thorn in the flesh was given to me, a messenger of Satan to torment me so I would not exalt myself. Concerning this, I pleaded with the Lord three times to take it away from me. But He said to me, "My grace is sufficient for you, for power is perfected in weakness."*

vs 7-9

On a purely human level where binary solution sets are the norm, it is tempting to look at this text and conclude Paul prayed for deliverance three times, and God told him no. Please note, however, that God does not say "no" anywhere in this text. He says, "But . . . " and then offers Paul the opportunity to live in a completely different paradigm from that of deliverance yes/no. I think we need to be very careful about inserting a "no" into this conversation, when that "no" is all too often a human expression of a binary set which misses what God is trying to unveil. Bottom line, where we add a "no," we miss the "but."

Please hear me out. This is not simple semantics. God is not denying Paul the deliverance he is seeking; God is offering Paul a whole new way to live that is holy. By holy, I mean wholly, completely, otherly, beyond the simple yes/no of being delivered from his circumstances. Let me attempt to explain this in purely human terms with an admittedly flawed illustration.

A young boy pleads with his father for a snow globe of Buckingham Palace, but his father says to him, "I will take you to London."

Now think about this. Did the father say "no" to the request for a snow globe? In the simple binary set of snow globe: yes/no, the son still does not have a snow globe. On the surface it looks like a "no," but the reality is that the father has not said "no," and it would be incorrect for us to insert one here. The father can still give the son a snow globe at any time. He has not denied the request for a snow globe, but has instead offered the promise of a much bigger experience in a much bigger world. If the son chooses to stay in the world of snow globe: yes/no and thus insert a "no" into his relationship with his father, then the issue here is not that the father is denying the son a snow globe but that the son is refusing the world that his father wants to show him. That is the problem of inserting a "no" where God has not expressed one. If we insert a "no" where the Father is saying something completely different, it is very hard for us to experience the Father's "yes" because our perceived "no" locks us into one reality, while the Father's "yes" is being expressed in a different reality.

Let's take this a little deeper. I believe that when God says, "My grace is sufficient for you, for power is perfected in weakness," He is moving from the specific to the general. Paul asks for God to demonstrate His grace and His power by delivering him from one weakness, but God offers Paul a continuous flow of grace in spite of all weaknesses. Paul asks for grace and power to be expressed in a moment, but God offers a new experience of grace and power for a lifetime. What God offers Paul is a continuous flow of grace, or grace after grace, which means that God is offering Paul an opportunity to live in a new revelation of God's self.

Here's the breakdown:

- The entire fullness of God's nature dwelt in bodily form in Christ[54]

- Jesus has fully revealed the glory of God

- God's glory is expressed in grace and truth[55]

- And from the fullness of Jesus we receive grace upon grace.[56]

So while Paul is asking for deliverance from a situation, God is offering Paul the opportunity to live a grace after grace life, which can only come from an ongoing revelation of the glory of God in Jesus who is the embodiment of the fullness of God's nature and the source of all grace. Is it any wonder then, that Paul, despite not being one of the 12, had the greater revelation of Christ?

So let me invite you to reconsider where you are inserting a "no," that you begin instead to find His "yes." All of the promises of God are yes in Christ, from whose fullness we receive grace after grace.

May we step into a new adventure where God holds open to us a wholly new revelation of grace and presence as we let go of our questions and try to discover His.

THERMOSTATS

*Then the LORD said to Moses, "Why are you crying
out to me? Tell the Israelites to move on."*

Exodus 14:15

First, the story.

Some time ago a young couple came up for prayer;
we'll call them, the Fosters. The infant they were fostering
was suffering from a number of physical deficits. As my wife
and I went to pray for this baby boy, I was overwhelmed by a
powerful sense of destiny. I told the Fosters essentially, that the
physical issues were symptoms of a bigger issue; the infant's
destiny was being contested. When I went to pray over the infant
I focused on proclaiming destiny rather than on healing the
deficits. That week everything changed. It was a miracle not of
healing, but of displacement, because destiny declared displaces
deficits' despair.

I am still learning from this. It is so easy for me to dwell on
the deficits and to pray, live, declare, etc., from the deficits.

And now, for another story.

Awhile back I spent two days at one of the most progressive public universities on the West Coast. I interacted with several people who were bright, polite, and helpful, but overall the atmosphere of the place was brooding and gritty and gray, and it had no song. The following day I was at one of the premier Christian universities on the West Coast. The difference in the atmosphere was amazing. I felt "home" for lack of a better word. The atmosphere was bright and peaceful. The whole time I was there, I could hear Chris Tomlin singing in the back of my mind, "All to Jesus, I surrender . . . " Today as I think about my week, I am reminded that despite the skills I have developed as a thermometer, this is not what I was created for. I was created to be a thermostat, setting the atmosphere, not merely measuring it. Just to make sure I got the point, when I got back into the car to drive home, I turned on the radio for the first time that day, and the song, "Wherever We Go"[57] by Newsboys was playing. It says in part—

> Wherever we go, bluebirds sing
> And the flowers bloom and the grass gets green
> It's a curious thing
> But it's just our thing
>
> Wherever we go, the bees behave
> In the treetops, squirrels smile and wave
> It's a curious thing
> And it's humbling
>
> Hands up, holler back here
> Let's throw this party in gear
> We brought the welcome mat
> Wherever we go, that's where the party's at

Which brings me back to this thought. The atmosphere in this country needs to change. But it is **not** the President's job, Congress's job, big corporation's job, or the media's job to set the atmosphere.

This job is ours.

When we focus on the deficits, the best we can hope for is to be good thermometers. If we are going to change the atmosphere of our nation, we have to learn to declare destiny rather than dwell in the deficits.

America has a destiny as a missionary nation. We are a going and a sending people. We are a generous people continually pouring out our own sweat, tears, and blood—lots and lots of blood—for the sake of others. This is who we are. This is our destiny; this is who we are meant to be as a nation, not just as the church of a nation. This is so written into the fabric of our nation that non-believers are moved by the power of a God-given destiny. We even have publicly and privately funded non-Christian agencies and institutions reflecting this destiny—USAID, Peace Corps, Ameri-Corps, Red Cross, etc., (the list is really, really long). But there is a problem. Destiny is a compelling force. Destiny is a mantle that must be taken up, must be contended for, must be sacrificed for, and must be carried forward. Wherever there is destiny unfulfilled, there is a vacuum, which will be filled by someone or something. God prospered this nation for the sake of its destiny. Wherever the church in America has relaxed into a misunderstood and misappropriated prosperity, it has let slip the mantle of destiny, allowing others to take it up and carry it forward without the church's influence. This has led to deficits. But rather than looking at deficits, let's consider destiny. Perhaps we don't have an immigration problem in this country; perhaps we have a missionary problem . . . where we have stopped going to the nations, the nations are coming to us. Is this problem or opportunity, deficit or destiny?

The atmosphere of our nation needs to change. We are the ones responsible for changing it. Not by our complaints. Not even perhaps by our prayers. Perhaps it is time to stop crying out and start moving on. The church of a nation is meant to carry the mantle of a nation's destiny, allowing the nation at large to partner with the church in pursuit of its destiny. Perhaps it is time for the church to stop partnering with those who proclaim our nation's deficits. Perhaps it is time for the church to stop relying on presidents and politicians (and horses and chariots . . .) to solve our nation's deficits. Perhaps it is time for the church to take up the mantle of our nation's destiny, to contend for it, to sacrifice for it, to carry it forward. When the church of America has taken the lead in carrying our national destiny forward, then perhaps we will discover what it means to be thermostats rather than thermometers.

If we want to change the atmosphere, we must not dwell in the deficits. Stop crying out (over the deficits) and move on (into our nation's destiny).

Destiny declared displaces deficits' despair.

KINGSMEN

For just that reason, to keep me from being arrogant, I was given a thorn in the flesh, a messenger that Satan sends to cudgel me so I won't get too arrogant. On this account I three times prayed the Lord to make it go away. And I have been told: "Enough that you have My grace: power is perfected in infirmity."[58]

had been listening to an audiobook story of Fitz Chivalry Farseer, the son of a dead father and an unknown (and unwed) mother. Bad enough to be a bastard, but Fitz's father, Prince Chivalry, had to abdicate his position of "king-in-waiting" on account of Fitz's birth and then was subsequently murdered so that Fitz is tossed into the streets at the age of 6. It is at this point that his grandfather, the king, secretly chooses him as a king's man, and puts him in the care of the stable master, who gives him a place to sleep among the king's horses and hunting hounds.

Not having grown up in the political intrigues of a feudal

society, I really don't know what it means to have the grace of
the king or to be the king's man, but this story is helping me to
gain some insight. Within his own heart, the heart of the king,
and only two others, Fitz is "the king's man." But in the public
arena, he is only "the bastard" (among the nobility) or "the dog
boy" (among the street folk). He grows up struggling against his
circumstances and frequently tries through his own efforts to
rise up and be his own man only to be challenged by his mentors,
"Are you a king's man or aren't you? Remember that you are not
the player, you are the tool."

And so I came upon this re-translation of II Corinthians 12
from the original Greek "Enough that you have my grace" which
in the context of my fictional story comes across as "Enough that
you are a king's man." You see, grace is not so much a mystical
force that is flowing from God to Paul to magically make him
feel better. Grace is the state of the relationship between Paul
and God—Paul is a king's man; he has the king's approval, and
it is enough.

Perhaps this would be intuitively understood in the days
when kings ruled the earth and were addressed in public as,
"Your Majesty," but intimately as, "Your Grace." To have the
king's grace is to be in his favor, to have his approval, to be
"owned," named, or acknowledged by him as a king's man. In
Fitz's story it does nothing to change his daily reviling as the
bastard or the dog boy. In fact, in some ways it makes it worse.
If Fitz were not the king's man, he would be free to determine
his own destiny. Being the king's man means he is bound to the
king's service and thus bound to the place and the time where he
is outwardly just the bastard or the dog boy. And so the struggle
for Fitz is always in his own mind to understand that regardless
of his circumstances he is a king's man, and it is enough that
he has the king's grace. As a little boy in a big world, he has no

understanding of what that grace means, no perception of the hidden hand of the king moving to ensure that he is fed, clothed, housed, educated, trained, and shaped for the king's service. He has only his faith in the king and his knowledge that he is a king's man; which brings me back to Paul.

Having read through the Corinthian letters recently, I am struck again with the idea that leadership in the Kingdom of God means embracing the idea that we are not the player; we are the tool. This seems like a bitter pill to swallow at times. Leadership in the kingdoms of this world is about rising up and taking charge to be the mover and the shaker. But the greatest in God's kingdom are not the movers and the shakers, but the moved and the shaken. To be a king's man means being bound by the service of the king to a particular place and time, even when it is a place of suffering and a time of reviling. It is in those places and those times that we must remember that our Savior King knows what it feels like to be the bastard and the dog boy, and He showed us what it means to a king's man as He humbled Himself by being obedient even to the point of death on a cross.

If you find yourself bound to a place of suffering and reviling today, may I challenge you with this question: "Are you a king's man, or aren't you?" For me, the temptation of that place is always just to walk away, to be done, to be my own man, to chart my own course, to determine my own destiny for good or for ill. But then I hear His voice again: You are mine . . . you are mine . . . you are My own treasured possession.

I know that come what may, I have His grace, His approval, His favor, and His heart, and whatever else I am, I am a King's man.

COMFORTER

D id you grow up with the King James Version of the Bible? I labored with that for years. I remember when the New International Version first came out; it was like a cool breeze on a muggy day. A couple of years ago, my wife and I went to Scotland and stood in the church where King James was crowned. Everyone around us was speaking English . . . I think. I could barely understand some of them. It reminded me that English is hardly a homogeneous language, and the English that the King James Version was written in is not the English we speak today. If I use the word "comfort" or "comforter," what comes to mind today? Is it a hug after a hurt and the reassurance that it will be okay? Is it being wrapped in a big blanket with a cup of cocoa? We often associate "comfort" with ease, and a "comforter" with one who consoles, quiets, pacifies, or soothes.

But words have changed. The word "comfort" comes from the Latin word, *confortare*, which became, "com-fortis," and then eventually, "comfort." It literally means, "with fortitude." Fortitude is courage in the face of pain and adversity. Back in the day of King James, when John 14:16 was translated into

English, "comforter" meant something more than we generally think it does today. A "comforter" was one who came alongside with fortitude. A comforter was one who gave strength and hope, and provoked one to a place of strength in the face of pain and adversity.

I had an encounter with the Comforter recently. I was really despairing, frustrated, weary, overwhelmed, wanting to give up—I know you, too, have been there at some point. In the back of my mind, I began hearing Bryan and Katie Torwalt's song, "Sing Holy." Despair threatened to overwhelm me, but from within was this constant repetition of, "Sing holy, sing holy, sing holy . . ." When I joined in that song, I found that while the problem was not resolved, I was. That is the work of the Comforter. He's so amazing. He did nothing about my circumstances (at least as far as I can tell), but He did something with me. You see, the old English word, "comfort," has more to do with provoking than it does with consoling.

Later that morning, as I lay on the gym floor gasping like a fish out of water, my gym coach, Teri, came over and grabbed me by my arm and put me back on my feet with a huge grin that I knew was saying, "You can do it." That's more of what "comforter" meant back in King James' day. The comforter is the parent who brushes the dirt off you and puts you back up on the horse, bicycle, balance beam, or whatever it was for you. The comforter is the one who picks you up after you've fallen or been knocked down, and puts you back into the game. The comforter is the one who steps into the middle of your, "I can't go on," and says, "YES WE CAN!" The comforter is the one who says, "Come on . . . we got this. Put one foot in front of the other and just don't quit." But that's the catch: to receive the *com-fortis* of the Holy Spirit means we have to do something; we have to live with fortitude.

The deception of self-centeredness is such that people often don't want comfort; they want pity. What is the difference? Pity is the enemy of comfort. Pity demands nothing from you; comfort demands a response. Pity paralyzes; comfort activates. Pity silences; comfort gives voice. The deceiver wants us wrapped up in pity and hungering for more. The Comforter wants us released into grace and hungering for more. Living on the right side of the cross means breaking free from pity and embracing the comfort of the Holy Spirit.

> *Every good gift and every perfect gift is from above, and comes down from the Father of lights.*
>
> James 1:17

> *And the peace of God, which surpasses all understanding, will guard your hearts and minds through Christ Jesus.*
>
> Philippians 4:17, NKJV

As we embrace the Comforter, we need to recognize that healing grace is a gift. The peace which we do not understand, but which guards our hearts and minds, is a gift. And if we've been given a gift, then we need to open it and use it. If we have received the comfort of the Holy Spirit, then when tragedy strikes, at some point grieving must come to an end. Even if others are still shaken and grieving, we don't have to be, and we don't have to feel guilty or conflicted that we are not. But we do need to understand that our gift is not for us alone.

I think perhaps there are three phases of receiving from God: apprehension (receiving), comprehension (revelation), and impartation (giving away). First, we need to apprehend that

God is presenting a gift to us and we need to lay hold of it. Second, we need to understand that wrapped up in every gift is a revelation of the giver. Whenever we receive God's gifts, there is an opportunity to step into a greater revelation of who He is. Finally, having received His comfort, grace, and peace, and having understood the revelation that accompanies the gift, we now have something to impart to others, and we need to look for opportunities to do so.

I think we often stop at simply receiving the gift. We have to be intentional and stay engaged in the process if we want to move beyond receiving to revelation and impartation. If we do not go all the way through the process, then the gift is just a gift for the moment. We receive it in the moment and move on from the moment. In a sense, the gift can be used up and gone. But if we go through the process, then the gift becomes a renewable resource in us. The gift is for the moment, yes, but the gift is also the key to a revelation that allows us to impart the gift to another. The act of imparting the gift to another then solidifies the revelation of the giver in us, which in turn gives us continuing access to the gift.

Never feel guilty about having received a gift, but never settle for receiving the gift only for yourself; freely receive/ freely give is one of the greater keys to the Kingdom. And when tragedy strikes, don't deny the comfort of the Holy Spirit; embrace it.

COMPANIONS

I f we do not control our language, our language will control us.

I was reading through Hebrews 6:4 the other day in the HCSB version and was caught by this statement—

". . . became companions with the Holy Spirit . . ."

Think with me for a moment about what it would mean to become a companion of the Holy Spirit.

Why "companion of" and not "partaker of" or "sharer in" as the KJV and RSV or the NIV and NLT render it? Whenever we are trying to discover the theological meaning of a Greek word, it is always best to find the same Greek word used in a mundane or ordinary way. In Luke 5:7, we find this same Greek word (bold print emphasis):

*They beckoned their **partners** in the other boat to come help them.*

The use in Luke 5 helps us see that this word means, "partners, companions, associates."

Now this is where the issue of language becomes important. Language changes over time. Maybe "partaker of" meant something more to people 400 years ago, but today we typically partake of things, not people. We have a share in things, not people. Today the language of partaking/sharing allows for an objectification of the Holy Spirit that has become a tragic norm in many believer's lives, but "companions of," now that is a different story. Another issue with language in this verse is that if I think of myself as partaking of/sharing in the Holy Spirit, then the language allows myself to be the center or the focus of the activity. Please note, however, that this verse in Hebrews 6 does not say that Holy Spirit has become our companion rather that we have become His companions. The language here insists that He is the center and focus of the activity.

So what does it look like to become a companion of the Holy Spirit? The answer to that question will help us to unravel another significant question: "What does it look like to be 'led by the Holy Spirit?'"[59] I think the answer is simple; it looks just like Jesus and the disciples. Even as Jesus revealed the Father,[60] He revealed the Spirit.[61] Jesus said that there would be another (of the same kind) that would take His place, so I see in the disciples' companionship with Jesus the picture of our companionship with the Holy Spirit. The twelve started their journey as Jesus' disciples, but they became His companions. Jesus went about doing His Father's business, teaching and healing and demonstrating the Kingdom of God. He led; the disciples followed. Jesus taught them, imparted to them, and they became His companions in His work. The Holy Spirit leads;

we follow (ideally). He teaches[62] us, He imparts[63] to us, and we can become His companions—not partakers of, or sharers in, but companions. Think of it this way: He became my comforter so that I could become His companion.

That is a story worth telling.

COVERING

pretty much grew up in church, so I feel like I can say that I've seen it all—the good, the bad, and the ugly. I saw the ugly once again as a church person was using social media to accuse someone else in church of wrongdoing and encouraging others to re-post, re-tweet, etc. I really wanted to jump into the Facebook string, but my wife wisely reminded me that it was not my place . . . but I really, really wanted to say something. So I'm going to vent to you, my patient, reading friend..

This really is an area of repentance for me because I am an investigator by vocation. I can feel a "cover-up" in my bones, and it just makes me want to dig and dig until everything is exposed. I am a black and white, wrong or right, night and day kind of guy. It's a bit hard for me to say these things because it goes against my nature, but here is the bottom line question: How do I deal with sin and conflict in the church? First, I think I need to freely confess that I used to be a "What you do in secret will be shouted from the rooftops" kind of person, but now I have a new set of guiding principles that I am struggling to make real for myself.

1) Love covers, hate exposes.

> *Hatred stirs up conflict, but love covers over all wrongs.*

Proverbs 10:12

I know, right? It doesn't get much more black and white than that. I think very few people would admit to hating the pastor/elder/brother/sister whose sin they feel they need to expose, but that's pretty much the line the Bible seems to draw on this subject. So whenever I feel a need to expose someone's sin, I need to stop first and very seriously examine my own motivation.

> *Whoever would foster love covers over an offense, but whoever repeats the matter separates close friends.*

Proverbs 17:9

What am I hoping for? Whenever I feel a need to expose someone's sin I need to stop first and very seriously consider the desired outcome. What do I want the end result to be: love and fellowship, or strife and division? Again, the Bible seems to be, unfortunately, quite clear on the matter.

> *Above all, love each other deeply, because love covers over a multitude of sins.*

1 Peter 4:8

But really, what are we talking about here? I mean, this can't mean that we should be covering up sin. After all, it is sin, right? Maybe this just means we should be tolerant and forgiving. Can't I expose someone's sin while still loving and forgiving them? That's a good question, actually. Can I? Can you? If so, you are a wiser, kinder, gentler, more deeply spiritual man or woman than I am.

2) What would Jesus do?

There is more than one side to every story. One day Jesus caught a bunch of people in the act of exposing sin (we commonly refer to this story as "the woman caught in adultery"). Here are the three sides to this story: the exposers, the woman, and Jesus. Jesus confronted the exposers, but He covered the woman. Here's the moral of the story: only one person was drawn to Jesus' side, and it wasn't the exposers.

Am I being soft on sin in all this? Doesn't sin need to be confronted and exposed? Maybe. I don't know. I do know this: none of us is without sin. The reality is that God, in His loving-kindness, has a daily exercise of covering my sin for the sake of drawing me to His side. Before I do or say anything when I see sin in someone else in the church, I need to seriously consider whose side I want to end up beside: their side, my side, or Jesus' side.

3) Guard your heart.

> *Guard your heart above all else, for it is the source of life.*

> Proverbs 4:23

I have decided that there is a connection between this verse and Philippians 4:7:

And the peace of God, which surpasses every thought, will guard your hearts and minds in Christ Jesus.

The connection between the two is that I have to guard my own heart in order for God's peace to guard my heart as well. Here's how:

Whatever is true, whatever is honorable, whatever is just, whatever is pure, whatever is lovely, whatever is commendable—if there is any moral excellence and if there is any praise—dwell on these things.

So these are my new guiding principles. This is still really hard for me. It really goes against the grain, yet that is why I am convinced it is the right way. Maybe it's time we all got in on the greatest cover-up in history.

DYING

Easter was just around the corner. But it was not an empty cross or an empty grave that had captured my attention; it was an empty mattress.

We got the call in the morning; our neighbor had passed away. As I stood looking through our kitchen window, I saw his empty mattress leaning up against the side of the house. Two days before, my wife and I had stood by the side of that mattress while James Stewart was still lying in it, struggling to breathe, but indomitably cheerful. I was grieved then, but when we got the news of his passing, I was relieved, because while death is a non-issue to me—indeed to anyone in Christ—dying can still be a difficult process. So this morning as I reflected with gratitude upon the empty mattress, I had a new thought: Jesus did not just die for me (a moment), He also experienced dying for me (a process). The thought I actually had—because I make up words whenever I feel the need—is that Jesus did not just die for me, He "dyinged" for me, too.

I understood why the Protestant and the Catholic crucifixes are different. However, I wonder if perhaps by excluding the

Catholic imagery of Jesus' broken body twisted and nailed to a cross, we have lost the reality of how Jesus transformed not only the moment of death, but also the process of dying. We know that for those of us in Christ, eternal life has already begun and that to be absent from the body is to be present with Christ.[64] On Easter Sunday mornings we all celebrate Christ's resurrection, and hopefully we are all reminded that physical death holds no fear for us anymore. Death has been swallowed up in victory, this we know, but who among us does not look forward to the process of dying with some trepidation? Death is easy; dying is hard work. The process of dying can be lengthy, messy, painful, and ugly. I have watched people dying, and while I don't fear death, the truth is, I really do have a fear of dying. Maybe to be precise, I should say, I have a fear of dying poorly.

I heard someone teach that having taken on our humanity, Jesus could have died from any cause, and He still would have been resurrected, and thus, He still would have broken the power of death over us. An interesting thought, but I think the empty mattress tells a different story. If Jesus had died any other death, such as beheading (which the Romans did in those days), or stoning (which the Jews did), then I think the professor was right: Jesus still would have been resurrected, and death would still have been swallowed up in victory.

But what about dying? Dying, I fear, would have remained unchanged, as Jesus would have passed swiftly from this life to the next, leaving us to live in fear of an experience that He, Himself, did not go through. But because of the way that Jesus died, He not only died for me, He also *dyinged* for me. He fully experienced the *process* of His body slowly failing: breathing becoming increasingly difficult, heart pounding harder and harder, vision fading, hearing dulling, pain becoming all-consuming until He felt trapped, suspended between life and death, unable to live, yet unable to die. That, my friends, is what I fear (am I alone in this?). But Jesus went through that process on the cross so that He has transformed dying in the same way that He has transformed death. I know now that if Jesus died for me, then He also dyinged for me. I know now that if I have died with Christ, then I have also dyinged with Him. This means that I do not need to fear the process of dying any more than I need to fear the moment of death; it's been done, and done well.

Now I know that when my day comes, if I keep my eyes on Jesus, I, too, can experience dying, and do it well.

So take heart dear ones, and come Easter, let us celebrate the reality that Jesus has conquered not just death, but dying. As for me, if my dying turns out to be a long and painful process, please put a good old-fashioned Roman Catholic crucifix where I can see it so that I can be reminded that my dying has already been caught up in His.

DEATH

I sleep, but my heart is awake. A sound! My love is knocking!

Open to me, my sister, my darling, my dove, my perfect one.

Song of Solomon 5:2

Behold, I stand at the door and knock . . .

Revelation 3:20

Imagine yourself swimming underwater in a murky lake. You can't see clearly. You can't hear clearly. Every movement is resisted. Your body aches from the cold. Your lungs burn with the effort of holding on. Can you feel it?

Now imagine yourself swimming underwater a really long time—your entire life, actually. It's all you've ever known—the heaviness of limb, the ache of the body, muffled hearing, the cloudy vision. Can you feel it? Suddenly, you see a light. You swim toward it, and in a moment of transition, you break through the surface and find yourself standing on a sun-drenched beach, warm and dry. You are breathing warm air, spicy with pine, and sweet with lavender. You see a bright sky that goes on forever, with colors sharp and clear. You hear a symphony of wind blowing in the trees, birds singing in the bushes, insects moving in the grass. All of your senses are enhanced beyond imagination. You walk, and then run, moving without resistance, without pain, feeling strength that you've never felt before as you begin to realize that you have just entered the world that you were created to live in.

Now imagine that what I just described is what it feels like to die.

I think that for those who are in Christ, death is not the Grim Reaper who comes to us to tear our souls from mortal bodies, but the Boy Scout who pulls us to the surface of a murky lake, drags us out of the water onto the beach, and stands us up on our feet. As believers, we talk about how death has been defeated and how the sting of death has been removed. Why, then, do we still fear it? Why do we still act as if death is our enemy? Why do we struggle against it, fighting it like a drowning man fights his would-be rescuer? Why do we not see death as an old man/old woman's friend?

These are not rhetorical questions.

I was reading John 10:2-3 recently.

> *The one who enters by the door is the shepherd of the sheep. The doorkeeper opens it for him, and the sheep hear his voice. He calls his own sheep by name and leads them out.*

I was going to write something about our role as doorkeepers with the keys to the Kingdom. I was going to write about our role in opening doors for Jesus to come into our homes, our workplaces, our cities, and our nations, because it seems to me from Revelation and Song of Solomon that sometimes Jesus will not go through a door that is not opened to Him. I was going to write about what it means to be watchmen, doorkeepers, and intercessors, and how when Paul asked for prayer that doors be opened for him, it is possible that in his mind he was thinking something far more significant than we think. All that would have been good and is worth thinking about it. Maybe I will return to it one day.

But this morning as I slept, my heart was awake, and I dreamed of a large family sitting around a table discussing their mother's imminent death, while the mother lay alone in another room of the house. A man named John stood in the hallway between the one room and the other. In my sleep, I thought to myself, *Why aren't they in the room with their mother opening the door for her?* Do you see it? John wrote that the doorkeeper opens the door so that the shepherd can enter and lead his sheep out. As I lay there sleeping, I remembered a friend telling me that in his mother's last days, when she was not physically responsive to the natural world, she was still physically responsive to the spiritual world. When they prayed in her room, she prayed. I remembered the story of my friend who was already "walking on the beach" before his physical body ceased to function. I remembered the numerous stories I have read over the years of people whose deaths were very much a "crossing over" as they were still able to express with their physical bodies what their spirit was experiencing. And it made me wonder, what does it mean to be a doorkeeper?

We talk about changing the atmosphere through our prayer and our worship. We talk about open heavens. We talk about thin spaces where heaven and earth intersect. What if the thinnest place we could experience in this lifetime is the place around the bed of a dying believer? What if the "openest" heavens we could experience in this lifetime is at the moment the door of heaven is opened and the Good Shepherd enters the room to lead His beloved out? What if being doorkeepers means that we have the authority and the ability to transform dying in the same way that Jesus transformed death?

These are not rhetorical questions.

I have stood by and watched as people died. I wonder sometimes if Jesus is standing outside the door and knocking desiring to enter in so He can lead His beloved out, but He can't, because family and friends have barred the door, piled furniture up against it, and plugged their ears to the sounds of His calling. What if instead of denying and resisting the process of dying, we were to gather around the bed of the dying one as if we were stepping into the thinnest of all places on this earth? What if we changed the atmosphere of the dying room by our prayer and by our worship? What if two or three people gathered in worship around a dying person could experience Jesus in their midst? What if they could actually open the door?

These are not rhetorical questions.

What if, instead of trying to hold the door closed, we could open it?

The one who enters by the door is the shepherd of the sheep. The doorkeeper opens it for him, and the sheep hear his voice. He calls his own sheep by name and he leads them out.

Death has been defeated; perhaps dying can be as well.

ENOUGH

Give us this day our daily bread.

Matthew 6:11

For Demas has deserted me, because he loved this present world.

2 Timothy 4:10

Black Friday. What a concept. Is there any other country in the world where people express their national gratitude by rushing out to spend money they don't have on stuff they don't need?

Today I offer you more questions than answers. If you're not grappling with some of these questions yourself, then either you already have the heart of St. Francis, or perhaps you're living a little closer to the edge than you realize.

What does it mean to have enough? What does it mean

to prosper? Why was I conceived in the country that controls/consumes most of the world's resources? What am I meant to do about it?

Solomon in all of his wisdom was not wise enough to survive being wealthy. Demas, despite having been a traveling companion of Luke and of Paul, was not spiritual enough to avoid being entangled by the things of this world. Even King David, with his heart after God, got so used to getting whatever he wanted, that he stretched his hand out beyond the boundaries that God had set for him.

What if the reason that God does not answer my "give us this day" prayer in the way that I want Him to is because He is more concerned with answering my "lead us not into temptation" prayer?

Our heavenly Father knows our hearts. He is *for* us. He is the giver of all good things. Is earthly treasure a good thing for us? Is it possible that our finances are limited by God because He loves us, and He does not want us to go the way of Solomon or David or Demas? It is possible that there are flaws in my character that I am yet unaware of that would lead me down the path of ruin if I got used to getting whatever I wanted?

James offers us two reasons for unanswered prayer:[65]

1) You do not have because you do not ask,

2) You do not have because you ask amiss, so that you can spend it on your own pleasures.

Is it possible that I have established the boundaries of my own finances by how and where I spend my money? Have I become so obsessed with my own creature comforts that God will not grant me increase because He knows I will only spend it on me and mine, and thus travel one step further down the path that Demas trod?

Try this little exercise with me. Think back for a moment. What have I done in the past when I have received a raise, a bonus, a surprise windfall of money? What did I do with that unexpected bounty?

What if "Our Father" is serious about **us** being the body of Christ, the family of God, a charismatic community that perfectly reflects the image of the Trinity as persons in relationship? What if **our** Father answers, "Give **us** this day **our** daily bread," as a body rather than as individuals? In America, our thinking has become so skewed by the concept of the individual that we naturally presume that whatever comes into my hand must be for me first. What if that isn't true? What if **our** Father answers the prayer of "give **us** this day our daily bread" by giving one person just enough, one person not enough, and one person more than enough?

Is this not what the nation of Israel demonstrates to us? God blessed some with abundant fields, vineyards, and orchards, while others He blessed with, well, with what did He bless them? Did not Jesus say that we would always have poor people with us? What provision did God make for the poor? Was it not the same abundant fields and vineyards and orchards that He blessed others with? Do you see it? God raised up wealthy men and women, and blessed the work of their hands so that their fields, vineyards, and orchards produced more than enough, and then gave them specific instructions to insure that the poor had access to their "more than enough." God answered the prayers of everyone all together by giving some more than enough while allowing others to have not enough so that all together would have enough.

Think about that for a moment please. What if in God's household, His economy, He has put some of His children in a place where they always have more than enough, and some of His children in places where they will never have enough? If that is the economy of God, then what happens when those who have more than enough begin to redefine "enough"? Is it possible that the reason America's economy is struggling is that as Americans, we have allowed God's economy to struggle?

I know these are a lot of questions. I am just asking so that if you are not already grappling with these questions, you would begin to do so. Let us not forget that the deceitfulness of wealth can choke out the Word of God in our lives. The wisdom of Solomon, the heart of David, the companionship of Luke and Paul—none of it was enough to protect against the deceitfulness of wealth. We are soaking in a spirit that is besotted with the deceitfulness of wealth and the desire for material things. Are we so much wiser than Solomon? Do our hearts burn for the presence of God more than David? Have we surrounded ourselves with better brothers and fathers than Luke and Paul? Wealth, the "more than enough," is deceitful. If we are not aware of it, if we are not engaged in the struggle against its deceit, we will be carried away by it.

Our Father, give us this day our daily bread, and lead us not into temptation.

PROSPERITY

What is prosperity? Perhaps it's as simple to define as this: prosperity means having enough. The problem is how do we define "enough"? The first part of this problem is that in our consumer culture, we tend to define "enough" by our lack rather than by our sufficiency. I don't have _____ (something I want), therefore, I do not have enough. The second part of this problem is that in our human need for certainty, we define "enough" as that which makes us feel secure. The final part of this problem is that we define prosperity functionally as that which we produce, possess, or consume rather than relationally as who I know. What if the secret to prosperous living was simply in allowing God to define for us what is enough?

After humanity's sin, God said that the earth itself was cursed so that we would "eat bread by the sweat of our brow." I used to think that sweat tied back to the idea of hard labor, but I have seen a couple of word study/commentaries recently that say the "sweat of our brow" is not the sweat of hard labor, but the sweat of anxiety. I am quite sure that if Adam and Eve worked hard in the Garden prior to sin, they experienced sweat, as sweating is simply a natural process of intelligent design. The "sweat of our brow" that became part of the curse is different; this is the prickly sweat that breaks out on a person's forehead when they are anxious or afraid. The effect of the curse is that mankind, having lost our relationship with God, now labors and lives in the fear of the uncertain future. Today I have enough, but will I have enough tomorrow? The curse is such that we are constantly living in the fear of lack. We cannot even enjoy what we have today because we are so anxious over what we may not have tomorrow.

We may miss the impact of God's promises to prosper Israel because we can always drop into the local grocery store and get some food. It's December as I write this and about 15 degrees Fahrenheit outside; yet I think nothing of eating fresh grapes and strawberries for breakfast. I did not have to get up in the cold and dark to go stick my hand under a chicken in order to have eggs for breakfast, nor did I have to milk a goat or a cow. I did not have to scoop grain from a dwindling supply to make my daily bread. I think very few of us in our culture understand what it means to have to work the soil and grow our own food, living season by season with nothing to fall back on, knowing that we are helplessly dependent upon countless variables. Will there be enough (but not too much) rain? Will it fall at the right time and in the right place? Will there be insects or diseases? Will it be too cold at night or too warm during the day? Will the processes of pollination via wind, ants, or bees, be sufficient? Will what we have be stolen in the end? So for the subsistence farmer, there is no rest. There is only work, uncertainty, and anxiety, unless. . . .

What if prosperity were relational, not functional? What if prosperity were not about how hard we worked or how much we had, but about who we were in relationship with? Perhaps the blessing of prosperity is qualitative, not quantitative. Perhaps true prosperity is not about how much we have or don't have. You could have a million dollars in the bank, but if you are still living out of a sense of lack, you are not prospering. You could feast on $10,000 tins of caviar spread on $10 crackers, but if you are still eating it by the sweat of your brow, you are not prospering.

I believe God wanted Israel to prosper. His promise to them was that if they lived in proper relationship with Him, He would ensure that enough rain fell at the right time and in the right place so that they (corporately) would always have enough. The true blessings of prosperity are the peace and the rest that can come only to one living in a relationship of trust with the Creator, who alone gives bread for the eater and seed for the sower.[66] Prosperity for Israel was never about economic security; it was about relational security. God alone was the provider, sustainer, and defender. God's prosperity has never been about achieving a natural certainty through personal or public wealth; it was, and is, about living in a persistent relationship of trust with the Creator/Provider in the midst of consistently uncertain circumstances.

So what about us? Does God want us to prosper? I think so, but the question again is how we think about prosperity. Is it primarily functional or primarily relational? When Adam and Eve were in the Garden of Eden, they had a relationship with God and a relationship with the land. When they broke their relationship with God, God broke their relationship with the land so that at times, their best efforts would produce thorns and thistles.

Jesus said to not be anxious about what we will eat or what we will wear because our Father knows what we need. In other words, He knows what "enough" for us is. When Jesus says in

Matthew 6, "Do not be anxious,"[67] it is a direct renunciation of the curse of Genesis 3:19, "By the sweat of your brow you will eat." This is not a breaking of the curse on the land—creation itself is still groaning in frustration and futility—rather, it is a restoration of our relationship with the Creator, so that despite uncertain circumstances, despite even the thorns and thistles that can spring up after our best efforts, we no longer have to live under the power of the curse. The rest (lack of anxiety) that Jesus proclaims for us is not based on a removal of uncertainty via financial security. It is based on the removal of the need for certainty that the curse produces in us. It is about moving out of the functional and into the relational because the curse only has power in the functional realm. The only way to be completely free from the effects of the curse is to learn to live from the relational (seek first the Kingdom) into the functional (all these things will be added).

Now, let me get back to the idea of what is "enough" for us. I believe Jesus promised that we would all have enough, yet the fact remains that many believers have "more than enough" while many more have "not enough." This is a fact of history from Israel's covenant with God, to the first generation church of the New Testament, until today. The poor have always been with us, and the some of the poor have been us. Perhaps part of the problem here lies in our Western individualistic mindset, which can radically misinterpret the gospel at times. What we are missing is that Jesus, a person in relationship, was speaking not to individuals, but to persons in a kinship culture where property was not owned by individuals, but held in trust for the family.

Jesus says:

> *So do not worry, saying, "What shall we eat?" or*
> *"What shall we drink?" or "What shall we wear?"*
> *For the pagans run after all these things, and your*

heavenly Father knows that you need them. But seek first his kingdom and his righteousness, and all these things will be given to you as well.

We as individualists hear Him speaking to us alone, as individuals, or at best, to us alone, along with our spouse and children. Perhaps what we should be hearing is this from the NTV Bible (my own New Texan Version!):

Your heavenly Father knows that y'all need them. But seek first His Kingdom and His righteousness, and all these things will be given to all y'all as well.

There is a profound difference between the idea that "all these things" will be given to **me** as an individual, and the idea that "all these things" will be given to us as persons in relationship. You see, if God's prosperity is primarily a relational issue, then prosperity must have its way in all of our relationships, not just our relationship with God. God's promise of "enough" is not to me alone, but to me as a person in relationship with others, so that wherever believers truly comprehend the nature of the body of Christ, there will always be enough for every part of the body. God is forever trying to build of us a community, a body, a family, a temple for His dwelling place, and wherever adding "all these things" to an individual will serve to increase individualism and decrease community, He's not going to do it.

When we learn that God adds "all these things" to persons rather than to a person, we can see how prosperity builds community. So for us to find rest from the curse, we must find a new way of living and a new way of thinking—not just about God, but about each other as well.

EXCEEDING

was struck by a little thought that unfolded into something much bigger. I heard this morning, as I have so many times before in Sunday sermons, "God will meet your needs," but for the first time ever, in my head I heard, "No, He won't."

Here is why.

When someone says, "God will meet your needs," what some of us hear is, "God will (just barely) meet your needs." Some of us have a poverty mentality that affects our perception of who, and how, God is. Some of us have such a narrow idea of stewardship and such a strong drive to be responsible that we can actually end up denying the generosity of God. We read, "Give us this day our daily bread," and we picture a meager loaf of something hard and dry doled out to us one day at a time. What I was confronted with this morning was my measure of God and how I have allowed, "God will meet your needs" to evoke pictures of a communist bread line rather than of my mother's kitchen.

Jesus said:

> *Give, and it will be given to you; a good measure—*
> *pressed down, shaken together, and running over—*
> *will be poured into your lap. For with the measure*
> *you use, it will be measured back to you.*

Luke 6:38

Allow me to focus in for a moment on the measure that we use. With what measure do I pray, "Give us this day our daily bread?" With what measure do I measure God? Is He austere, or is He extravagantly generous? Now have a pause. Take a moment. What do you *really* believe?

A friend of mine was watching Oprah Winfrey one day. It was one of those episodes where she had put on a lavish display for all of the ladies, gifting them with cars, or diamonds, or something over the top like that. My friend heard God say to him, "I am more extravagant than Oprah Winfrey." Can Oprah Winfrey out give God?

Jesus said:

> *If you then, who are evil, know how to give good*
> *gifts to your children, how much more will your*
> *Father in heaven give good things to those who ask*
> *Him?*

Matthew 7:11

When Jesus fed the 5,000, how many full baskets were left over? When Jesus fed the 4,000, how many baskets full were left over? When Jesus turned the water into wine, what did it taste like? When Jesus said, "Throw your nets on the other side," what was the catch like? You see where I am going with this? With the measure I use, it will be measured back to me.

Compare my measure to God's measure. Paul wrote that God would supply all of the Philippians' needs. Note that Paul does not say God would "meet" their needs, but that He would "supply" their needs. With what measure would God supply their needs? Philippians 4:19 tells us it would be "according to his riches in glory."

James writes:

Every generous act and every perfect gift is from above, coming down from the Father of lights; with Him there is no variation or shadow cast by turning.

James 1:17

John writes that God gives the Spirit "without measure".[68]

Think about these three phrases:

- "According to his riches in glory"
- "How much more?"
- "Without measure"

Many of us still think we are living in a zero-sum game. If you are not familiar with the term, a zero-sum game is any situation in which the sum is always zero. This means for one person to gain, someone else has to lose so that the sum of all is always zero. Most Americans, including a lot of Christians, believe that economics are a zero-sum game. Therefore, if the rich gain, the poor must be losing. That is why as we approach election seasons, we will see fiscal liberals openly and unashamedly talking about their plans for wealth redistribution.

I say that a lot of Christians still believe in the zero-sum game because that is what our giving reflects. Our giving reflects a zero-sum game controlled by an austere God who promises to (just barely) meet our needs. In the back of our minds there is little voice always telling us, "If I give so that someone can have more, then I will have less." But here is what we need to embrace (not just understand): with God, life is not a zero-sum game. This has been illustrated in the Bible over and over again. Isaac, for instance, planted crops in the middle of a famine and reaped 100-fold. Even with modern farming techniques available today, in a good season we get only 40- to 50-fold returns. Isaac got a 100-fold return . . . in a famine.

With God, there simply is no such thing as a zero-sum game. Twelve full baskets left over. Did it cost anyone? Did anyone lose in order that others might gain? What about the little boy who gave his five loaves and two fish? Having once been a little boy, I am quite sure that he ended up eating far more than the five loaves of bread and two fishes that day. God has never stopped being the Creator—the one who makes something from nothing. Life with God is simply not a zero-sum game, and it is time to stop living like it is.

God will not (just barely) meet our needs; He will always exceed them. Final proof?

Now the One who provides seed for the sower and bread for food will provide and multiply your seed and increase the harvest of your righteousness.

2 Corinthians 9:10

Why? Because God is generously, extravagantly, and always lavishly good. When we seek first the Kingdom of God, all of life ceases to be a zero-sum gain and instead becomes a display of the glorious generosity of a God who has never stopped being the Creator, the Father of lights, from whom every generous act and every perfect gift flows.

So let me challenge you with this. The next time you hear someone say, "God will meet your needs," stop and say (to yourself), "No, He won't; He will exceed them!" Then go out and live life like you believe it.

ERGONOMICS

Moses saw that though the bush was on fire it did not burn up.[69]

There's a lot of burnout in helping people. Like the bush that caught Moses' attention, we were meant to burn but not to burn up, because anything that burns up, will burn out. Ministering to people is work, and work requires energy. I'm not just talking about vocational ministry. I am talking about the work that all of us are called to and should be engaged in: loving our neighbors, bearing each other's burdens, healing the sick, restoring those outcast from community, breaking the grip of the demonic, proclaiming the Kingdom of God, building one another up, maintaining hope, etc.

We were created in Christ Jesus to do good works.[70] We have been and are being equipped for works of ministry.[71] That word, "work," in the Greek is, *ergo.* If you remember your high school physics, then you know that today we still use the erg as a unit of measurement to define "work," where, Work = Force x Displacement. In other words, work is accomplished when some amount of force is applied to something so that there is some measure of displacement. This word *ergo* is the same word used when Paul writes to Timothy and urges him to "do the work of an evangelist" in order to fulfill his ministry.[72] It's the same word used when Paul says that the person who desires to be an overseer desires a noble work. Ministry is work. Work uses energy. Where does that energy come from?

Ergonomics (simplified) tells us that burn out has two basic causes: a person is doing the wrong work or a person is doing a work the wrong way. It is the same for spiritual ergonomics.

There is a difference between a candle and a lamp. It is this difference that is the answer to the question of why some people burn out and others don't. A burning candle consumes its own substance where a burning lamp does not. A candle is the fuel; a lamp has the fuel. Some candles are small and burn out quickly. Some candles are huge and burn brightly for a really long time. The reality of all candles, however, is that they will all eventually burn out. A lamp can be filled and refilled. It can continue to burn even while being refilled.

So if you are feeling burnt out right now, think about this: Are you a candle or a lamp? It's really a critical question because we have the capacity to be either one. Many, many people are living as candles. They burn up until they burn out. They burn out on their vocation, on marriage, on parenting, etc. Sometimes they can successfully reform themselves from the drips and puddles of leftover wax; sometimes they can't. Every candle eventually comes to the end of itself. If you're burning out right now, I don't want you to feel any condemnation. I'm writing this to you as one who has lived most of his life like a candle in the wind. I want you to know the hope of our calling—we were meant to be lamps, not candles.

So where does it start, this journey to lamp-hood? I think it starts, oddly enough, with a stop. Stop giving of yourself. Most people think there are two kinds of people in the world: takers and givers. Actually there are three kinds of people in the world: takers, givers, and receivers. The difference between a giver and receiver is that one is a candle and one is a lamp. The candle gives out from itself while the lamp gives out from what it receives from another.

Jesus began His ministry on earth by receiving,[73] and despite all of the need that surrounded Him, He continually pulled away from opportunities to minister just a little bit more so that He could receive from the Father.

When Jesus sent out His disciples, He did so with these words:

Freely you have received, freely give.

Matthew 10:8

After His resurrection, He told His disciples to wait. What an odd way to start turning the world upside down. Jesus has already declared that all authority in heaven and earth has been given to Him, and He has already sent them into the world with a "Go", so why did the divine "Go"[74] become a divine "Wait"? They waited because they had His authority, but they still needed His power. So they waited until they had received,[75] and then they went. This "power" they were waiting for according to Acts 1:8 is the Greek word, *dunamis*. It is literally the dynamic energy which is required for human persons to do divine work without burning out. Without this power, we are candles, not lamps.

In Ephesians 1, Paul prays for the church to have enlightenment so that we would know "the immeasurable greatness of His power to us who believe, according to the working of His vast strength."[76] The word "power" again is the dynamic energy necessary to do work. A literal translation from the Greek to English[77] says it is "the overcasting (transcending) greatness of the power of him into us . . ." Then in Ephesians 3, Paul prays that we be "strengthened with power by his Spirit in the inner man."[78] Again a literal translation puts this as "into" the inner man. The dynamic energy of God is being conveyed by the Spirit of God into our inner man so that we have the power to do the work without the work consuming us.

God's desire for us is that we would experience His love in such a way that we would be "filled with all the fullness of God"[79] so that we can be lamps and not candles. Paul says that being filled comes as a result of knowing the love of Christ in a way that transcends knowing. More than anything else, that means receiving.

I've been a taker. Picture me holding tightly to what I have with one hand while grasping for more with the other.

I've been a giver. Picture me with both hands reaching out to others.

I want to be a receiver. Picture me with one hand reaching out to the Father while the other hand reaches out to others.

It starts with learning to receive from His presence in stillness. From there, it grows into learning to receive from His presence in busyness. Ultimately, it grows into the ability to receive from His presence while giving from His presence into His purpose. This is what it means to be lamps, not candles, and to burn brightly for Jesus in the work of the ministry—whatever that looks like for you—without ever burning up or burning out. This is the hope of our calling.

FAITHFUL

*Now without faith it is impossible to please God,
for the one who draws near to Him must believe
that He exists and rewards those who seek Him.*

Hebrews 11:6

Comparisons are odious.

—my mother

Let me tell you a little story. Well two, actually.

A man is called by God to go into a city and preach. His public ministry is fruitless In fact, he preaches for 40 years without success. He dies in obscurity having been removed from the place of his calling and ministry.

How shall we judge this man? Would you spend your time and energy supporting his ministry? Would you invest in this man as a friend and companion in the Kingdom? Would you give your money to support his ministry?

A man is called by God to go into a city and preach. His public ministry is amazingly anointed. In fact, he preaches for 40 days, and the entire city converts.

How shall we judge this man? Would you spend your time and energy supporting his ministry? Would you invest in this man as a friend and companion in the Kingdom? Would you give your money to support his ministry?

Now for the punch line. If you chose to invest your time, energy, and money in the ministry of the second man, you may be sorry.

The question I put before you today is who was faithful to God's heart—Jeremiah or Jonah? You see, it is man who looks on the outward appearance, but God who looks on the heart.

It is faithfulness to the heart of God that pleases God. The author of Hebrews does not say, "Now without success it is impossible to please God." It is our faithfulness that brings God pleasure. Man judges us based on our "fruit," and we often judge ourselves based on our "fruit." Again, we tend to define "fruit" based on outward appearance. For us to judge fruit in this way is a difficult thing. Ultimately, it is God who gives the increase anyway, and if we focus on fruit as the criteria for judging success or failure, we may find ourselves judging God.

Fruit is a tricky thing. Jesus healed 10 lepers, yet only one returned to give glory to God. Will you judge Jesus by the fruit as we judge others or ourselves? Jesus healed thousands of people. Jesus set many people free from demons. Jesus raised people from the dead. Where were those thousands of people who felt His touch, ate His bread, received His blessing, and knew His love when He was hanging on the cross? Will you judge Jesus by the same standard we use to judge ourselves and others?

My dear friends and companions in the faith, do not allow yourself to get sucked into the trap of comparing your work in the Kingdom of God to another's. Do not look to another man or woman's success as a measure of your own. They are them, and you are you. The criteria which God judges you by—the one thing that is necessary to bring him pleasure—is faithfulness.

So let me urge you, if you feel like all you have to offer to God is your faithfulness, it is enough. Set aside your comparisons. Set aside your evaluations. Set aside your metrics, your performance standards, and your expectations.

Set your heart on being faithful to God's call on your life. It is enough.

FATHER

Our Father.

As two of the most significant words that Jesus ever spoke, these two words simultaneously confront the sin of every culture, and at the same time contain the entire hope of the gospel. When we truly understand who Jesus is, and that He fixes His gaze on us, and says simply, "Our Father," suddenly we are caught up in Him into the greatest story that can ever be told. Think about it just for a moment. We were strangers, enemies, slaves, orphans, lost, and dead in our sin. Then Jesus came to us, looked at us in all of our sin and said, "Our Father." And lest we miss what He has done for us, He presents us before our Father, calls us His brothers and sisters, and gives us the Spirit of adoption to enable us to say with Him, "Abba, Father."

Do you see the power of these two words as the hope of the gospel? I cannot escape them. They haunt my waking hours and echo through my dreams. I drive down the street and see the homeless beggar on the side of the road, and I hear "Our Father." I see the pictures of bodies strewn like refuse in the wake of ISIS, or the Burmese Army, or the mobs of India, or Pakistan, and I hear, "Our Father." I see the bloody hands of the murderers themselves, and I hear, "Our Father." The world is looking for something to unite us, some common thread of humanity—this is it. How could the world change if we, as followers of Jesus, would learn to look on others as Jesus looked on us and speak this out as both prayer and promise, "Our Father"?

But Jesus' words also confront every culture. "Our Father" is a slap to the face of the Western world where we have exalted the individual self beyond all reason. The "American Dream" is fundamentally flawed because at its foundation lies the myth of the self-made person. It is hard for us to realize that the concept of the individual is barely as old as this nation we live in, yet it has become the prevailing paradigm of the empowered and enfranchised so that the gospel itself has been twisted into something significantly less than what Jesus died for. But my culture is not the only one that is confronted by "Our Father." These words confront all other cultures as well; but I cannot speak to them as well as I can to my own. Allow me to offer two specific examples.

My heart was broken one afternoon when I was watching a video about the nuclear disaster in Fukushima, Japan. A farmer was being interviewed about the effect of the ambient radiation on his farm. The story was supposed to be about the long-term poisoning of the food supply, but it took a sudden turn and became for me about another poison that has been set into the fabric of what it means to be Japanese. The interviewer and a Japanese farmer were walking through a greenhouse talking about radiation levels in the food he was growing when the farmer led the film crew to a rock under a tree. He explained that this was the spot where his father had hung himself when he found out that the produce he had been selling for the previous two weeks had been contaminated by the fallout from the reactors. Shame is a poison that so cripples the Japanese psyche that suicide is the only answer. The pressure in Japan to drown the person in the sea of society is absolutely sinful. But when Jesus says, "Our Father," He offers a new way of seeing oneself as a person in relationship.

In a similar way, the caste system of India, which says that one is born Brahmin, and another is born untouchable, is absolutely sinful. But Jesus confronts the sin of the caste system as He holds out one hand to the Brahmin and the other hand to the Dalit and says to them together, "Our Father."

Wherever you are in the world, the message of the gospel is about "Our Father." It is not that I now have a personal relationship with Jesus, but that I have been caught up into Jesus' personal relationship with God. There is a bigger story going on here and "Our Father" invites us to step into it.

US

As I have been allowing the words "Our Father" to have their way in me I am beginning to come to conclusions in some areas and to ask some troubling questions in others. When I read the prayer that Jesus opens with "Our Father," one other word leaps out at me—"us."

> Give *us* our daily bread.
> Forgive *us* our sins
> Lead *us* not into temptation.
> Deliver *us* from the evil one.[80]

Having grown up as an individual in the West my first realization is that I don't even know what these words mean. I simply do not have the proper grid, and so, I need to repent. I need to learn to change the way I think just to be able to properly hear what Jesus is saying.

I have been letting my imagination wander for some time now regarding the imagery of personhood offered in the Bible. Psalm 1 and Jeremiah 17 likens a man who trusts in God to a tree planted by streams of water. Ezekiel pictures a stream of living water coming out from the temple of God; Jesus declares that out of each of us will flow streams of living water; Paul says that we are each one a temple of God. So I am both a tree planted by a stream and a temple from which a stream is flowing. How does that work? Well, frankly, as a Western individual, not very well. But as a person in relationship in the Kingdom of God, it is a beautiful picture.

I have friends who know and love Jesus. From each one of them is flowing a stream of living water. If I plant myself as a tree and send my roots towards what flows from their lives, I am assured that I will prosper. Likewise, as my friends root themselves as trees next to the stream of living water that flows from me, they will produce good fruit. In this way, we are absolutely interdependent and connected one to another.

Now think about this picture in terms of the prayer, "Lead **us** not into temptation." What hope I find as a tree in realizing that dealing with temptation is not "my" problem, but "our" problem. What weight of responsibility I feel as a temple of the Holy Spirit when I realize that my brother's temptation is not "his" problem, but "our" problem. This is what I am learning. When I am struggling with temptation, I need to send my roots towards the stream where I can find what I need. When I struggle with my ego, I send my roots in relationship towards the man who embodies the servant heart of the Father. When I struggle with my faith, I send my roots in relationship toward the man who embodies the power and the authority of the Spirit of God. When I struggle with my lack of compassion, I send my roots in relationship towards the man who embodies the compassion of Jesus. When I struggle with my sexuality, I send my roots in relationship towards my wife first, and towards my closest man friend whom I trust. Do you see it? "Lead **us** not into temptation" means something far more than I have realized.

So this week, as you are rooted and grounded in the love of Christ, would you begin to stretch out your roots towards another and pray this prayer with me? "Our Father."

MERCY

One night as I went to bed, I was reading a devotional that randomly popped up via email. The author's point was that "Lord, have mercy" is the most-often prayed prayer in the Bible. He talked about how the closer we draw to God, the more we are aware of our need for mercy. One of his key points was that the "closest" you could get to God in those days was what we call in English, "the mercy seat," which was at the heart of the tabernacle. This devotional set my mind racing down old patterns, and then new.

Probably like many of you, when I hear "mercy," I think, "not getting what I deserve," because that's what most of us were taught. Unfortunately, this is too small an idea and can cause us to dramatically miss the point. In the Bible, I find no exclusive linkage between sinfulness and the need for mercy. Mercy does not belong primarily to the person-as-sinner/God-as-judge set. That kind of thinking is the result of our Western mindset forcing foreign ideas over the top of ancient Eastern words. Mercy actually belongs to the person-as-subject/God-as-king set, and that changes things.

Let me explain. If mercy is simply "not getting what I deserve," then what place does mercy have on this side of the cross? Certainly I can see the need for mercy on the other side of the cross, but if I am a dearly loved child of God, a sanctified saint, a brother and co-heir of Jesus who is caught up in the Beloved and seated in heavenly places with Christ, dressed in His righteousness alone, being transformed from glory to glory into the image of Christ, filled with the Holy Spirit, etc., then why should I be concerned about "not getting what I deserve"? If mercy is "not getting what I deserve," then why would I, in my current precious, treasured, bought-with-a-price-state need to obtain "not getting what I deserve" at the throne of grace?[81] If mercy has to do with not being punished for my sin, what do I have to do with sin anymore? If I still need mercy today in my current state, then what good was the cross?

If mercy is "not getting what I/you deserve," then why is it the high priest could only approach "the mercy seat" once a year, and even then, he went in with a rope tied around an ankle so that just in case he was struck down in judgment, his dead body could be dragged out? Does that sound at all to you like "not getting what you deserve?" Think about it for a moment, to approach "the mercy seat" was to risk receiving exactly what was deserved. How is that mercy?

So then, what were all of those Hebrews in the Bible asking for when they pleaded for God to show "mercy," or to be "merciful"?

Well as usual, the language is what has gotten us into this trouble, so the language is where we have to go to sort this out. Bottom line, either the words in the Old and New Testament that were used to translate into English as "mercy" do not mean the same thing as we understand the word "mercy" to mean, or we do not fully understand the meaning of the English word "mercy." And hey, guess what? It's both.

If you read through all the uses of the word we translate "mercy" in the Old Testament in a literal Hebrew/English translation, you do not see "mercy." Rather, you see variations of "gracious" or "compassionate." The primary Hebrew word that we translate as "mercy" rarely has a direct connection to sin or to offense. It is simply the act of a superior bending or stooping to an inferior in kindness.

Mercy primarily has to do with a subject gaining an audience with his Lord. God as sovereign has no obligation to interact with His subjects. For Him to do so in any way is an act of "mercy." This is the case in the Eastern mindset specifically. When God walked with Adam and Eve in the Garden of Eden prior to sin entering the world, it was an act of "mercy." The "mercy seat" in the tabernacle was not the place where people did not get what they deserved; it was simply the place where the Sovereign Creator bent in kindness to meet with His creation.

What about the New Testament? It's the same story. If you look at a literal translation in the places where we expect to find "mercy," we actually find variations of "compassion." The Greek phrase, *kyrie eleison*, meaning, "Lord, have mercy" (literally translated, "Lord, have compassion"), is actually very helpful because it demonstrates that the idea of "mercy" is not linked to God as judge. Rather, it is linked to a subject coming to his Lord, his sovereign, seeking an audience so that he can, then, ask for a favor. The request for mercy is about gaining an audience. It is the subject speaking to the sovereign and saying, "Have compassion on me. Grant me an audience, and allow me to ask you for a favor."

This is most clearly demonstrated in Mark's account of the healing of the blind man. "Have mercy on me"[82] is the request to Jesus for an audience with Him. Having granted the audience (there's the mercy), the Son of David then asks His subject what he wants, and the subject then requests a specific grace (favor, or boon) from the Son of David.[83] Do you see it now? Mercy is Jesus granting an audience to the blind man. The man, then, having obtained mercy (the audience), now has an opportunity to request a favor from Jesus, which he does. He then finds grace in being granted his sight. An Old Testament equivalent is when Esther obtained mercy in being granted an audience with the king and then found grace in the King's response to her request to save her people.

So how have we been missing this one? Well I think part of what we are missing is that at some point in the history of religion, the meaning of the English word, "mercy" was hijacked by those who insist on living on the wrong side of the cross. There is more than one meaning of "mercy," even in the English language; *Merriam-Webster* gives us three. There is the one definition that we are all familiar with: "forbearance shown especially to an offender or to one subject to one's power", i.e., "not getting what we deserve." Two other meanings are "a blessing that is an act of divine favor or compassion," and "compassionate treatment of those in distress." It is the latter two, which satisfy the intent of the majority of uses of "mercy" in the Old and New Testaments.

When are told that we can approach the throne of grace with confidence and obtain "mercy,"[84] we are not talking about obtaining a "not getting what we deserve." We are talking about obtaining a compassionate response, a condescension, a bending or stooping from the King of the universe in kindness toward us. We are simply talking about gaining an audience, like Esther did, and like the blind man did. I do not have to come trembling in fear before the throne of grace seeking mercy because of an awareness of my sinfulness or my shortcomings. I need to settle that once and for all. Either my sin and my shortcomings are now a non-issue when I approach the throne of grace, or the cross means nothing.

I think the closer we get to God, the more aware we are of His majesty, His greatness, His goodness, His infinitude (yes, that's a real word), and thus, the more aware we become of our need for mercy. Why? Because we know we need Him. We need face time with the King, and that requires His mercy. It requires that He bend to meet us. If I come to the King of universe, I need mercy, simply because His person is vast beyond my comprehension. For me to even think to approach Him means that He must in His kindness bend to meet me, or I am lost. Not lost like sin-lost, but lost like being tossed overboard in my skivvies in the middle of the Pacific Ocean on a moonless night in a typhoon, and being told to find my own way back to Seattle-lost.

"Lord have mercy" is the most often prayed prayer because it is simply a request for an audience. If I gain an audience, that is His mercy. If He acknowledges my presence and listens to my request, it is His mercy. It is just that simple. This is why the author of Hebrews says we can obtain mercy and find grace.

"Lord have mercy" is a request for an audience, and for a compassionate response, and it is a request that is always answered now that we are in Christ.

Because we have His attention continually, what grace, what favor, what boon will we ask of Him? "Lord have mercy" is a great opener for a prayer, but if we repeat it more than once in the face of His invitation to step forward and find His grace, then we are actually denying the audience that Christ died to give us. So now when I read the author of Hebrews' instruction to approach the throne of grace with confidence so that we can receive mercy and find grace, this is what I am now hearing and what I hope you will now hear as well.

So lift up your eyes to the hills, dear ones! Where does your help come from? You can seek help from this King or from that governor or from this president or that mayor and you may or may not gain an audience (mercy), you may or may not get a hearing (mercy), they may or may not pay you any attention (mercy). But God is merciful. When you approach His throne, He will bend low, He will draw near to grant you an audience; He will give you His attention. Then, having obtained mercy, what grace would you have from Him in your time of need?

GRACE

have been caught up more and more of late with the idea of grace. This passage in particular has my attention more than any other at the moment:

> *The Word became flesh and took up residence among us. We observed His glory, the glory as the One and Only Son from the Father, full of grace and truth.*[85]

> *Indeed, we have all received grace after grace from His fullness.*[86]

I am discovering in a new way that grace is not the opposite of sin or the response to sin. Grace is not the opposite of law. Grace is prior to law, prior to sin, prior even to creation. Grace is part of who God is. It looks like this: glory is revealed as grace and truth. If Jesus came to us full of grace and truth and "the entire fullness of God's nature dwells bodily in Christ,"[87] then the fullness of God's nature must be manifested in grace and truth.

Let's try this a different way. If we observe the glory of God in Jesus who is full of grace and truth, and Jesus as the image of the invisible God reveals the Father,[88] then the Father must be full of grace and truth.

Think about this with me for a moment. God does not change His nature. If His nature is full of grace and truth, then it has always been so. Jesus coming to us full of grace and truth is not God's response to our sinful condition; it is simply God coming to us in the fullness of who He is. What this means is that grace is as much a part of my life now as saint and son as it was when I was sinner and slave.

The righteousness of God is revealed from faith to faith. As we are learning to be led by the Spirit of God and to walk by faith rather than by sight, we find ourselves becoming more and more dependent upon the graces of God. It is true that there is a step in maturity in learning to worship God simply for who He is, but let's be cautious about getting too religious on this point with ourselves and with others. It can make us sound really mature and spiritual to talk about seeking God's face and not His hands. But let's be honest. If we are really walking by faith and not by sight, then we are going to be totally dependent from day to day upon "every generous act and every perfect gift"[89] that comes down from the Father.

Every gift of God is a "grace." The Greek word, *charismata*, literally just means "graces." He is the gifting-God, and we need the graces He offers. We are even told that there is a place we can go to find the graces that we need:

> *Therefore let us approach the throne of grace with boldness, so that we may receive mercy and find grace to help us at the proper time.*

Hebrews 4:16

Would it not be terribly silly for us to get all religious about "seeking His face and not His hands" when we are invited to boldly seek what God has for us? We are talking about gifts here, manifestations of the grace of God. The language in Hebrews 4 "at the proper time" ties in very neatly with the language in James, "every perfect gift," because the word "perfect" means that which is mature, complete, ready for this moment of time in this particular place. It means that as you walk from faith to faith, regardless of where you are and what is happening, there is a grace for you, a gift of God that is particularly fit (mature, ready, complete) for the time and place you are in. If we are going to walk by faith, we need to learn one simple phrase: There's grace for this.

We need to allow these phrases to dominate our responses so that walking by faith becomes an exercise in seeking and finding the grace that God has for us in any situation.

I find it interesting that we "receive" mercy, but "find" grace. Here's the deal: you cannot find what you are not seeking. When you step into a new level of faith or a new "unknown," the grace that you need now may not look like the grace you have previously found. That's why you must find it again. You may be in so deep that you think there is no grace for you, but there is; you just don't know yet what it looks like. Keep looking with all of the assurance that, from the fullness of Jesus, we are receiving grace upon grace.

Let me leave with you something I hope will change your perspective forever.

Immediately I was in the Spirit, and a throne was set there in heaven. One was seated on the throne, and the One seated looked like jasper and carnelian stone. A rainbow that looked like an emerald surrounded the throne. . . . Something like a sea of glass, similar to crystal, was also before the throne.

Revelation 4:2-3

A jasper stone is typically a dark blood red, and a carnelian is a smoky orange. If you look west across the ocean at the setting of the sun, you can see the sky turn to a dark smoky orange and then to a deep red, and then sometimes, just for a moment, you will see a bright green flash. Why? Because the heavens declare the glory of God, and every setting of the sun gives us a glimpse—as in a mirror—of the throne of God.

In heaven there is a throne of grace. John sees a throne set in heaven. John is seeing the throne of grace. The one seated on the throne (full of grace and truth) looked like jasper (a deep red) and carnelian (a smoky orange). From now on, every time you see the deep red and smoky orange of a sunrise or sunset, I want you to say to yourself, "There's grace for this." Let the daily declaration of the glory of God in creation remind you that there is a throne set in heaven, and the one who is seated on that throne is full of grace and truth. Let every sunset remind you that you have been invited to stand before that throne and find the grace that He has for you.

I don't know what you are facing right now, but let me be the first to tell you: There's grace for this.

HEALING

The hands of the King are the hands of a healer,
and so shall the rightful king be known.[90]

Once upon a time, a man owned a nice property with a river running through it. Most of this river was wide, slow moving, and smooth, but one part was steep and churned violently through heaps of rocks and narrow twisting channels descending into a whirlpool. The man fenced off the bank of the river in this area and put up a sign that read, "No swimming." He then told his son that he was free to swim anywhere in the river except that he must stay away from the rapids.

One day his son decided that the calm water was boring and the rapids looked exciting, so he broke through the fence and waded out into the rapids. He was, of course, swept off his feet, bounced off the rocks, and carried into the whirlpool where he was trapped, battered, broken, bleeding, and clinging desperately to a rock as the river tried to decide whether to beat him to death or to just drown him.

Upon hearing the cries for help, the man came along and saw the boy clinging to the rock. He stood on the bank and called to him, "Do not fear my son. You disobeyed me, and you broke my fence, but I forgive you."

The End.

Now tell me, what do you think of my little story? No? Okay, how about an alternate ending?

The man waded into the river and dragged the boy out of the water. The man then looked at his son, stripped naked by the force of the river, cradling torn hands together, limping on twisted ankles, blood running from his brow, scarcely able to breathe because of his bruised ribs and said to him, "Do not fear my son. You disobeyed me, and you broke my fence, but I forgive you, and have rescued you from your stupidity. Now follow me back to the house; you have work to do."

The End.

How about that? Better now? Of course not.

I think we are all familiar with Paul's statement in Romans 3:23, "All have sinned and fall short of the glory of God," but perhaps we are too familiar with it. We know that the Greek word translated as "sin" is an archery term that simply means to "miss the mark," but do we understand that, in context, this verse is not saying that we have simply "missed it." This is not an, "Oops! Try again;" this is an entirely hopeless situation. We have not just missed to the left or to the right, nor have we simply overshot the target. A literal translation of this verse would read, "All missed and are wanting of the glory," where "wanting" literally means, "to be later." *Strong's Concordance* tells us that by implication "to be later" can be read, "to come behind," or "to fall short." We are not merely missing the target; we cannot even reach the target.

Imagine me taking my Daisy classic spring-powered BB gun out to a rifle range and shooting at a target on the 300-meter line. Get the picture? Practice doesn't matter; discipline doesn't matter; intent doesn't matter; desire doesn't matter; aim doesn't matter. We just cannot get there from here. At a minimum, that's what this verse means. Sin is not just missing the mark as if we had a chance of hitting it. Sin is the absolutely hopeless inability to ever reach the target. That is why being forgiven for not hitting the target is not enough; something needs to be done to change the fact that on my very best day without Christ, I have no hope of even getting close to the target.

So why are we incapable of reaching the target?

If any of you have seen the movie 300, then you can get the picture easily enough. (The movie depicts Leonidas' stand against Xerxes at Thermopylae. I'm not recommending it, mind you—just using it by way of example.) Ephialtes of Trachis is dismissed by Leonidas, not for lack of courage or desire, nor for the strength and accuracy of his spear thrust. Leonidas dismisses Ephialtes because he is too small, too bent, and too twisted out of shape to hold a Spartan shield high enough to take his place in the Greek phalanx. No amount of courage and no amount of training can change the reality that Ephialtes, a severely deformed hunchback, is and always will be incapable of lifting a shield to the necessary height.

And so it is with us. We miss the mark because we are so wounded and bent out of shape that we are incapable of hitting the target even if we made the effort. The wounding often starts with something that was done to us. Just like bacteria in an open wound, if we let just a little bitterness, a little unforgiveness, a little doubt, or a little lust into the wound, it will fester and grow beyond the original hurt. Then the hurt itself becomes a source for further sin until we are locked into a vicious cycle and end up crying like Paul:

Who can free me from this body of death?

Romans 7:24

I think we fail to realize sometimes, how badly sin wounds us. Sin is punishing in its effect. The punishment of sin is such that not only the soul, but even the body can be wounded by it. Is it any surprise when the person consumed with bitterness, anger, or self-loathing, also has ulcers, high blood pressure, or autoimmune disorders?

Being in sin is like being caught in a raging river. We are battered and broken and trapped by the force of it. It is a catch 22. Sin wounds us, and then as a result of our wounding, we sin. So forgiveness for missing the mark is not enough; we also need to be healed.

This was Augustine's take on original sin (simplified). We have been wounded, and thus we sin. The sin that we sin wounds us ever more deeply so that we are incapable of anything but more sin. We need a savior, yes, but we need a particular kind of savior. Sin is a punishing force, and it wounds both soul and body leaving us broken and helpless, so that if Jesus were to simply come to us and say, "Follow Me," we would be forced to admit that we cannot.

The first time that God formally introduces Himself by name in Scripture, it is as Healer.[91] Jesus was named "Jesus" because "He will save his people from their sin".[92] "Save" is the Greek word, *sozo*, which means, "to rescue or to heal." The root of the word *sozo* means, "to be safe" or "to be well." So save/salvation, heal/healing, and deliver/deliverance are three separate words in our English translations and often three separate ideas in our heads, but there is only one word in the Greek, *sozo*, which means, "to rescue or to heal." Theologically, it is perfectly fair to render Mathew 1:21 as: You are to name Him Jesus, because He will heal His people from their sins.

When Jesus presented Himself as the Son of God, it was not primarily as the forgiver but as the healer. Jesus' coming to save His people from their sins did not start with forgiveness; it started with healing. His ministry was not first as great high priest but the great physician. A literal reading of Isaiah 53 tells us that He was "being wounded from transgressions," and "being crushed from depravities," just as we were. Jesus waded out into the river to rescue us, and thus He bore in His body the punishing effects of sin. He was battered by the force of the river. His hands were torn, His ankles were turned, His ribs were bruised, and His brow was pierced. On the cross, Jesus carried in His outer man the wounding, punishing effects of sin that we try to keep hidden in our own inner persons. The Jews, representing the wounded in all of us, took all of their bitterness, hatred, and anxiety and lashed out against the deliver, who in their minds had failed to deliver. The Romans, representing the wounder in all of us, took all of their bitterness, hatred, and anxiety and lashed out against this Man who demanded they turn from the might of their king and their god to serve Him instead.

So Jesus took upon Himself both the punishing of the wounder and the punishing of the wounded. In doing so, He did not just forgive them both; He made a way to heal them both. It is not by His stripes that we are forgiven. It is by them that we are healed, and so, according to the Catholic catechism, confession ultimately is about healing. When the priest pronounces, *Te absolvo a peccatis tuis* (I absolve you of your sin), it is not the grace of forgiveness that is released, but the grace of healing. James established a strong link between healing and forgiveness when he wrote:

> *Is anyone among you sick? He should call for the elders of the church, and they should pray over him after anointing him with olive oil in the name of the Lord. The prayer of faith will save the sick person, and the Lord will restore him to health; if he has committed sins, he will be forgiven. Therefore, confess your sins to one another and pray for one another, so that you may be healed.*

> James 5:14-16

Notice what we would consider a confusion of terms. The prayer of faith will save the sick. Again "save" is the word, *sozo*, which interchangeably means "to rescue or to heal." Those of us who grew up in Western educational systems like to think in categories, and so we naturally associate "save" with "sinner" and "heal" with "sick." James hopelessly (in our minds) conflates the ideas of healing and forgiveness because where we see different things, the Bible really only speaks of one thing.

Now please don't misunderstand me here. I am not saying that we are all just unwitting victims needing to be saved from our innocent mistakes, but I am saying that sometimes forgiveness is not enough. The good news is that forgiveness is not all there is.

When I was a young man, I was hurt quite badly by a person; that was the first wound. Over time, I processed that hurt by daydreaming of hurting that person like they hurt me. For me to indulge in that fantasy was sin and that sin wounded me even more. I realized that I needed to forgive and to be forgiven. I tried and I failed over and over and over again. I kept sinning in my own thoughts, so I had to keep going back to Jesus asking forgiveness for my sin and exercising my will to forgive. It was simply not enough because sometimes forgiveness is not enough; the wounds needed to be healed. I did not know this until one day God simply stepped in and healed the wounding (both done to me by another and done to me by myself), and in a moment it was all over for me. Now I know that Jesus is not just my forgiver, He is my healer.

When I am caught up in a mistake, I ask for and receive healing. In the times I find myself caught in a cycle where I constantly have to seek forgiveness for the same thing, I now understand that when forgiveness is not enough there is healing.

So if you find yourself struggling with an issue of sin in your life, it's time to break out of the sin/forgiveness cycle. Ask the Holy Spirit to help you look past your sin to what lies beneath. How have you been wounded? How have you wounded yourself? Then present that wound to Jesus the great physician and be healed.

HOPE

But we also rejoice in our afflictions, because we know that affliction produces endurance, endurance produces proven character, and proven character produces hope.

Romans 5:3-4

have been thinking recently about the entanglement of "hope" and "future." When I consider these two words together, inevitably Jeremiah 29:11 pops into my mind:

"For I know the plans I have for you," declares the Lord, "plans to prosper you and not to harm you, plans to give you hope and a future."

I have some concerns about the popularized usage of this verse as it is generally considered out of context, and thus links "hope" and "future" causally in an inadequate way.

It is easy to hope when one has a future; does that even require any faith? But how does one hope when one has no future? How does one hope when one has no job prospects in a failing economy? How does one hope when one's child is dying in intensive care? How does one hope when one has terminal cancer? If hope is causally linked to future, then how does one hope in the absence of future? I think perhaps what we may be missing is that there is a "now-ness" to hope that needs to be embraced regardless of future.

At issue is whether we root hope in a known or assumed future or whether hope can be rooted in the now-ness of one's relationship with God—**not** as it pertains to a future expectation of good, but simply in the nature of God as the one who is present. Seen in this way, one can hope in God even in the absence of future. As Habakkuk wrote:

> *Though the fig tree does not bud . . . yet I will rejoice . . .*

> 3:17-19

How do we have hope in the absence of future? Presence.

I think Paul's writing in Romans 5 suggests that it is not future that produces hope, but character. Hope is a now issue. Hope has more to do with the conjoining of my present and God's presence than with any future. Simply put, the now-ness of hope is that regardless of what one is going through, one is never alone. Consider the simultaneous denial of future and affirmation of presence in God's words to Paul, "It is enough that you have my grace." Paul writes:

> *We also rejoice in our afflictions, because we know that affliction produces endurance, endurance produces proven character, and proven character produces hope.*

How does character produce hope? It all goes back to the fact that because we have peace with God through Jesus, we have obtained access to grace so that we rejoice in the hope of glory. It is all about our present and His presence. We have been declared righteous now. We have peace with God now. We have His grace now. And so we endure hardships knowing that we are never alone. It is this enduring that produces character, and it is the now-ness of this proven character that produces hope in us. Hope of what? Hope of glory. What is glory? The manifestation of God's presence. So hope is grounded not in future but in the present reality of righteousness, peace, and grace that assure us of presence.

One of my most poignant movie memories came in the closing moments of "The Hunchback of Notre Dame." As the hunchback is clinging physically to a cornice of Notre Dame's roof and metaphorically to life itself, he gazes down at the rabid crowd shrieking for his blood and utters this heartbreaking question: "Why?" It is the last spoken word in this film.

There are two ways to walk in hardship. Like the hunchback clinging by our fingertips to a religious structure, we can break our own hearts wondering why. Did I do something wrong? Did I do something to deserve this? Did someone else do something wrong? Am I being punished? Am I being schooled? Am I being attacked? Why God? Why? Why? Why? But it is all hopeless. The other option is to walk through hardship knowing—knowing that we are righteous, we are at peace with God, and we have His grace. It is this knowing we are not alone that produces endurance, and it is the daily endurance of denying the why and embracing presence that produces character. It is this proven character that produces hope in us, not hope in future, but hope in presence. Thus Paul writes, "This hope does not disappoint."[93] In the now, God's love has been, and is being poured out in our hearts through the Holy Spirit. Hope does not disappoint because of what is happening now.

This is why the Proverbs says,

> *Hope deferred makes the heart sick . . .[94]*

To defer hope is to cut ourselves off from the love of God that is continually being poured into our hearts like a river of living water. The author of Hebrews says:

> *We have this hope as an anchor for the soul, firm and secure. It enters the inner sanctuary behind the curtain where our forerunner, Jesus, has entered on our behalf.*

> 6:19

The hope that character produces in us pierces the veil, not between present and future, but between present and presence, so that His presence becomes my present, and He becomes all in all.

So beloved, in this now, whatever your hardship may be, may you know the embrace of the God of all hope. May you experience a quantum of hope until His presence and your present become one.

GLORY

Dear friends, don't be surprised when the fiery ordeal comes among you to test you as if something unusual were happening to you. Instead, rejoice as you share in the sufferings of the Messiah, so that you may also rejoice with great joy at the revelation of His glory.

1 Peter 4:12, 13

For our momentary light affliction is producing for us an absolutely incomparable eternal weight of glory.

2 Corinthians 4:17

M any of us are familiar with these two passages from Peter and Paul, but let me ask you to step back for a moment and consider them in a new light. How many of us automatically assume that these passages refer primarily, or even exclusively, to a future glory? How many of us see this as a "not yet" aspect of the Kingdom of God? I want to think about this for awhile. Peter says we are supposed to rejoice (now) as we share in Jesus' sufferings (now) that we may also rejoice with great joy at the revelation of His glory. Is this now or is it not yet? Paul says that our momentary afflictions (now) are producing for us an absolutely incomparable weight of glory. Is this glory now or is it not yet?

Follow me for a moment.

Moses said, "Show me your glory,"[95] and God manifested His goodness to Moses and proclaimed His name over him. Here is a revelation of the glory of God for an individual, in a place, at a time. Then Jesus, the visible image of the invisible God, the light and life of the glory of God, rose upon us in an even greater revelation of the glory of God for a people, in a region, in a season of time. Do you see how the revelation of this glory of God increases from the one to the many?

Then Jesus, the one who came to make the Father visible, says this:

> I have given them the glory You have given Me . . .
> Father, I desire those You have given Me to be with
> Me where I am. Then they will see My glory, which
> You have given Me.[96]

Jesus says He has revealed the glory of the Father to some, but He wants to reveal His glory to all. Is this now or is it not yet? Jesus makes a relatively simple and direct statement; if we are where He is, then we will see His glory.

Again we need to stop and ask ourselves directly whether we are/I am assuming a not-yet aspect to Jesus' desire that we be with Him where He is. This is a really big deal because many of us read this primarily as a not-yet, and thus miss the possibility of the now.

The key is in this statement: "I desire those you have given Me to be with Me where I am." We know that Jesus is always with us, but are we now with Him, or is this exclusively a not-yet? Paul answers this quite clearly when he writes that God raised us up with Christ Jesus and seated us with Him in the heavens.[97] According to Paul, this is a now. Now we are seated in heavenly places with Jesus, therefore, now we are with Jesus where He is. Thus, now is the time when Jesus can reveal the glory of God to us and now is that time that we can rejoice with great joy at this revelation.

Now the revelation of God's glory that started with one person in one place in one time has been opened to all peoples in all places for all times. Perhaps this is why Paul also writes that as we are reflecting the glory of the Lord, we are being transformed into His image from glory to glory.

There is a Now-ness to hope. Our hope is not merely that what we suffer now somehow produces something for later. The eternal weight of glory is not about "some glad morning when this life is o'er"; it is for here, and it is for now. Suffering now can result in glory now, because for those of us in Christ, eternal life has already begun. Did not Jesus say that this is eternal life, simply to know God and to know the one whom God has sent?[98] Those who are in Christ now have eternal life now. Thus the eternal weight of glory has already begun to settle upon us. If we can just get our minds right in the moment, suffering now can result in a greater revelation of His glory now. How else is the whole earth to be covered with the glory of the Lord?

So do not give up hoping, and do not defer your hope to the not-yet because—

Even though our outer person is being destroyed,
our inner person is being renewed day by day . . .
For what is seen is temporary, but what is unseen
is eternal.

2 Corinthians 4:16-18

The eternal has already begun. Jesus came to make the unseen seen. Let us rejoice with great joy because if Christ in us is the hope of glory, then us in Christ is the hope of glory revealed.

KEDGING

f we are going to move forward despite adversity, we all need to learn the art of kedging. Kedging used to be a common practice back when square-rigged ships could not sail into the wind or simply could not make enough headway against a current. A kedge anchor was rowed out ahead of the ship and dropped into the spot where the ship wanted to be. The ship was then "warped" into position by winching in the anchor line thus dragging the ship up to where the anchor was. This process could be repeated as necessary to move a ship along.

This process was often used to warp a ship into a narrow harbor or river mouth or simply to put a very large ship into a very small spot, but it was also used to get a ship over a sand or mud bar. History tells us that in some situations where naval warships had to get over a known sandbar, they would intentionally run themselves aground and then kedge themselves over. Have you ever stood in the surf and felt the wave action pulling the sand out from under your feet? The same thing happens when kedging over a sandbar. The obstacle, the sandbar, is there, but as soon as the captain intentionally runs his ship aground and starts kedging his way over, the same waves that put the obstacle in his path to begin with will begin to wash the obstacle out from underneath him. That's the power of being anchored to something beyond yourself.

The writer of Hebrews says—

We have this hope as an anchor . . . which enters the Presence behind the veil . . .

6:19

What hope do we have? Keeping in mind that the context of Hebrews 6 reveals the links between hope, our inheritance, and the promise of God, I will let you answer that question on your own. I want to focus here on the art of kedging.

We live in the seen, but the Bible says that hope is an anchor that pierces the veil into the unseen where Jesus has gone before us. Hope is a kedging anchor that we can set in the unseen, in the Presence, and then use to drag ourselves forward.

Some of us just can't seem to make any headway. Some of us are just circling and circling trying to get around a sandbar. We want to avoid a problem, conflict, or obstacle, because we are afraid of getting stuck. The truth is that we are already stuck. We need to just go ahead and run ourselves straight up against the obstacle, set our anchor, and begin to drag ourselves over, knowing that as we do so, the sandbar will begin to dissolve under the pressure that we bring to bear on it.

I find it interesting that in the Bible version I am reading, Hebrews 6 is titled, "The Peril of Not Progressing." A kedging anchor is not about holding your ground. A kedging anchor is about making forward progress when everything is going against us or when there is an obstacle in our path. We have this hope as an anchor not to hold our ground, but to pull on in order to move forward. It must start with a determination to move forward. Through prayer, we allow the Holy Spirit to draw out our hope and set it as an anchor in the unseen realm of our future in God. Then through faith and follow-through (being led by the Spirit), we work the winch and tow ourselves up the line into the place that God has for us.

I wish I could your answer question, "What does this mean for me?" I can't. This is too personal. I just want you to have the picture and to understand that though this is hard work, it is doable. You have a way forward.

When you are under sail being carried along by wind, that's fun, that's pleasure, that's the way ships were designed to move. When times are tough and storms are raging, it's easy to ignore the peril of just being carried along. I've done it. I'm not judging anyone who is weary of trying to sail into the wind or against the tide. What I'm saying is that it's time to stop sailing and start kedging. It's easy to be carried along by wind and waves hoping that the storm will blow out or the tide will shift, but that can be a false hope. Winching a ship yard by yard up a towline to the kedging anchor is just plain hard work. It takes grit and determination, but sometimes it is the only way we can move ahead. I want to say it again—we can move ahead. God has given us a way forward.

Let me encourage you to begin to practice the art of kedging in your life. Sort out what this means for yourself. You are going to feel the strain between where you are and where you want to be. When you've set your anchor, the tension on that towline is going to increase. As it does, know that hope does not disappoint because the love of God has been poured out into our hearts.[99]

NOW

Joy to the world, the Lord has come!

O kay, stop right there.

How many of you have sung that song in the Christmas season?

How many of you believe what you are singing? (I'll give you a hint: I didn't. I'll admit it, and that's why I'm writing this.)

I've been struggling with something over the years. Here's my problem. I grew up in the "I wish we'd all been ready" generation. The older I get, the more I realize that the "I wish we'd all been ready" mentality actually stands in opposition to the "Joy to the world" mentality. At some point, I am going to have to choose between them.

The "I wish we'd all been ready" mentality assumes that everything is going to get worse and worse until Jesus catches up all the faithful in the Rapture. That's when things really get bad—basically, on earth as it is in hell. You know the details—

the four horsemen of the apocalypse, scorpion/lion/demon-thingies terrorizing the planet, etc. (Maybe preteens should not be reading the graphic novel version of Revelation?) The blessed hope of my church was that one day soon we would all be caught up and taken out of this wretched place before it got any more wretched. (God forbid that we should suffer in this world.) The only debate allowed was whether Christians would be taken out rare, medium, or well done—pre-, mid-, or post-tribulation. I recall one pastor jokingly saying, "I won't even eat Post cereals." When my only "hope" is that someday soon I will get to escape this mess (some of which I am undeniably responsible for making), where does that put me in relationship to the world that the Father so loved?

The song says, "Joy to the world," and I think it means now, not later. Why should we be proclaiming, "Joy to the world" now? Because the Lord has come—not "is coming soon" but has come. The song proclaims, "Joy to the world" now. The Lord has come now. Let earth receive her king"—now. Isn't the message of Christmas that "of the increase of His government and peace there shall be no end?"[100] The angels proclaimed "peace on earth and goodwill toward men" while we were still sinners.[101] Jesus came to proclaim the Lord's favor while we were still enemies of God.[102]

Somehow we've turned Jesus' message of "the kingdom of heaven is at hand" into "turn or burn." (Do you see my crisis yet?) Isn't the message of Christmas a message of rest to a weary world? Is the message "turn or burn," or is it, "Do not be dismayed, for Christ the Savior was born into this world to save us all from Satan's power when we were gone astray"?

John the Baptist and Jesus both came preaching that the Kingdom of God was at hand. Jesus taught His disciples to pray, "on earth as it is heaven." He then sent them out to preach "the

Kingdom of Heaven is at hand," and He told them to act as if the Kingdom was at hand by healing the sick, cleansing the lepers, raising the dead, and casting out demons. He told His disciples that they would do "greater works" after He went to the Father, thereby answering the question of how His government would continue to increase even after He left. He made His disciples ministers of reconciliation (making peace between people) and told them to go out in His peace with a message of peace, thus explaining how His peace would increase on the earth even after He left it. The glory of the Lord has risen upon us, and Paul says that we are being transformed from glory to glory, thus explaining how the glory of the Lord is going to cover the earth as the waters cover the seas.

How does this "of the increase of His government and His peace there shall be no end"-mentality, square with the "I wish we'd all been ready"-mentality? How can His government and His peace continue to increase if His body, the church, is convinced of the opposite and believe that things must get worse and worse before Jesus can come and whisk us all away?

So let me ask me/you/us. What if we are supposed to be preaching, "Joy to the world," because:

1) The Lord has come (now)?

2) The Savior reigns (now)?

3) God has entrusted me (now) with the responsibility of "no more let sins and sorrows grow"?

4) He has come to make His blessings flow (now)?

5) He rules the world with grace and peace (now)?

Listen, it is time for some brutal honesty here. Either this song "Joy to the World" is a "now" song, or it is a "not-yet" song. If it is a "now" song, then those of us who grew up in the "I wish we'd all been ready" camp need to shake ourselves off, repent, and start living in a completely different way in relation to both God and the world. If it's a "not yet" song, then we just need to stop singing it. Seriously, just stop. Otherwise, we're just serenading a sinking ship. If Jesus has not come to make His blessings flow here and now, and if He does not rule the world with grace and peace here and now, then things really are going to get worse and worse, and the best we can hope for is a quick rescue for ourselves and the folk we manage to take with us.

"Maranatha, come quickly, Lord Jesus" ought to be our prayer from moment to moment because we desperately need God to end this madness before any more babies are born into this brutal mess.

But if we believe that God has a message of joy for this world now, if we believe that He has come to make His blessings flow now, that He reigns now, that He rules the world with grace and peace now, then we need to get a grip, dig in, and commit to living on this earth as if it were the only one we will ever have. If He rules the world with grace and peace now, then "on earth as it is in heaven" needs to become our prayer, our sermon, and our lifestyle. "Maranatha, come quickly, Lord Jesus" still needs to be our prayer from moment to moment, but it has to mean something completely different. If He rules the world with grace and peace now, then the Holy Spirit being poured out on all flesh now means that when old men dream dreams, they are not dreaming about the sweet bye and bye, but they are dreaming about great-grandchildren who go further and do more than they ever could. They are dreaming of great-grandchildren who walk on water to reach an island where the gospel has yet to be preached. They are dreaming of great-grandchildren who break up funerals by raising the dead. They are dreaming of great-grandchildren who bring rain to drought-stricken regions and who stop the rain in flood-ravaged villages. They are dreaming of great-grandchildren who discover cures for cancers, who buy enslaved orphans from sex traffickers, who prosper in business to create jobs and industry where poverty once reigned, and who negotiate peace between nations. And yes, they are also dreaming of great-grandchildren who will look into the eyes of the person holding the other end of the spear and say, "Father forgive them . . . they don't know what they are doing." If Jesus rules the world with peace and grace now, and of the increase of His government and His peace there will be no end, then that is what it means for old men to dream dreams.

So that's my crisis. Do I want out, or do I want in? I think I am deciding that this is my field of beans and I'm not going anywhere; I'm not waiting for anyone to rescue me, and you can have my sword when you pry it from my cold dead fingers. With my last dying breath, I hope to be dreaming a dream of great-grandchildren who are doing all of the things that I lacked the faith to do. I hope to one day have a better hope than to simply be rescued.

LEGACY

How will I be remembered? Will I be remembered? What is my life message? Will I be remembered for what poured out of my life?

Here's the story.

> *As He was reclining at the table, a woman came with an alabaster jar of pure and expensive fragrant oil of nard. She broke the jar and poured it on His head. But some were expressing indignation to one another: "Why has this fragrant oil been wasted? For this oil might have been sold for more than 300 denarii and given to the poor." And they began to scold her. Then Jesus said, "Leave her alone. Why are you bothering her? She has done a noble thing for Me . . . I assure you: Wherever the gospel is proclaimed in the whole world, what this woman has done will also be told in memory of her.*

Mark 14: 3-9

Now think about this for a moment. Jesus said that wherever the gospel is preached, what this woman did will also be told as a memorial, a record, a reminder of her (that's the meaning of the Greek word). Because of what she poured out then, she is remembered now. This brings me back to my question, "Will I be remembered for what poured out from my life?"

The woman in the story is not the only person who is remembered. This event was a tipping point for Judas. The result is that we also remember Judas for what poured out from his life, and the contrast is offered up to us in precise and gory detail for a reason.

As a former criminal investigator, I see no discrepancies in the varying gospel stories of Judas' end. I see different witness accounts from different vantage points in place and time. In a nutshell, here is what appears to have happened. In remorse, Judas goes out and buys a field and hangs himself. He dies alone, unmourned, and untended. In contrast to Jesus, no one comes to claim his body. In time, either the rope breaks or the branch breaks and, as it says in Acts 1:18, if you were to translate the Greek literally word for word, "prone becoming he ruptures in the middle and was poured out." In other words, his body fell prone upon the ground, broke open, and his insides poured out. The religious rulers then, at some point, buy this now defiled field with the defiled money, and set the field aside for the burial of foreigners (who, of course, are all defiled according to the religious rulers since they are not of Israel).

Yes, this is all real and perfectly explainable by modern science. I have seen this happen first hand. Back in '96, I was recovering the body of a man who had hung himself. In the process, the body fell prone upon the ground, burst open, and the insides poured out just like in Acts 1. Gross, I know. I am sorry, but there it is, and it is there for a reason. The language used under the inspiration of the Holy Spirit is too precisely similar for it to be a coincidence.

Three people in this story are remembered for what poured out of their lives: the woman, Jesus, and Judas. Will I be remembered for what poured out from my life? If I am remembered at all, will I be remembered for a life from which poured the sweet fragrance of divine love or will I be remembered for a life from which poured the cloying, gag-inducing reek of corruption and death? That's the question Scripture confronts us with.

Many who follow Jesus are remembered well. Many who follow Jesus are not remembered at all. Some who follow Jesus are remembered, but not well. Now is the time to consider the question. Now, "Before the silver cord is snapped, and the golden bowl is broken and the jar is shattered."[103] Now is the time to consider my legacy. How will I be remembered? Will it be possible to tell the story of Jesus without mention of me? Or, will my life be so tightly bound to the life of Jesus that it is not possible to tell the story of all that Jesus did in my day and in my world without also mentioning me?

For too long in the church we have ignored legacy. Perhaps out of fear? Perhaps the fear of pride has caused us to focus too much on the ideal of the faithful servant and not enough on legacy. Perhaps we are too caught up in the ethos of "I'm just a wretched sinner saved by grace" to think about the legacy we could leave behind as princes and princesses in the Kingdom of God? God actually encourages us to pursue legacy—to consider the fragrance that will be released when the jar is shattered. The fact that Jesus prophesied this woman's legacy shows us that God approves of the concept. Also consider also Paul's words from Romans 2:6:

He will repay each one according to his works: eternal life to those who by persistence in doing good seek glory, honor, and immortality . . .

Remember that Paul was writing to the Romans who above all else sought immortality through legacy. Free Romans valued honor, and above else, they wanted to be remembered well. In the words of the fictional General Maximus Decimus Meridius, "What we do in life echoes in eternity." This is the air that a free Roman breathed. Paul does not confront this most deeply ingrained of Roman cultural values; he redirects it. By doing so, he implicitly approves of the idea of seeking for glory, honor, and immortality.

Ecclesiastes says that we should remember our Creator in the days of our youth. It is never too early to begin thinking about your legacy, because, really, who of us knows the day when the jar will be shattered? But let me offer this encouragement, it's also never too late to begin thinking about legacy. God is the redeemer and restorer who makes all things new, and in the end, even the broken husk of a man using his dying breath to plead, "Remember me . . ." is granted a legacy.

MONSTERS

Zombies and vampires and werewolves, oh my!

But if you bite and devour one another, watch out,
or you will be consumed by one another.

Galatians 5:15

Seen any zombies walking around your neighborhood recently? Vampires? Werewolves? No? Well what if I restate the question? Have you seen anyone walking around without life, trapped in the bondage of their own flesh, driven to consume others by pain and hunger they don't understand?

Have you seen anyone so driven by their need to maintain an appearance of life that they are constantly sucking the life out of others? Have you been around any changelings who most of the time live quiet ordinary lives, but occasionally transform into raging monsters that attack everything and anything?

Seen any of those recently? I thought so. Me too. They are everywhere.

Paul writes that when we walked in our flesh, we were dead in our trespasses and sins. Augustine wrote of sin as if it were a disease that brought a great sickness into the soul. Sin is a virus that infected Adam and with which we were all infected. The disease of sin leaves us in a less than human state where we are dead in our sin but seeking instinctively to infect others. Without the ability to fully express what it means to be human (Jesus was the first one to do that), we are left with nothing but a hunger to consume so that consumption becomes our core identity, and we do not think/care about who gets hurt in the process of feeding our hunger. People without Christ are walking dead. There really are zombies everywhere, and if you're not careful, they will bite and devour you.

Some people get religion which gives a semblance of life but cannot sustain life. They look good on the outside, they blend right in, their words are smooth and attractive, but they never quite step into the light. Inside they are full of unresolved hurts and needs that drive them to enslave others. If you let them, they will suck the life out of you. There really are vampires everywhere.

Some people have unresolved fear issues. In certain seasons, their fears boil up into anger or rage, which turns them into mindless animals which devour even the ones they love. There really are werewolves everywhere.

So, yeah, zombies, vampires, and werewolves, oh my! What can we do?

First, we need to deal with our own monsters. Am I driven by a need to consume? Am I trying to satisfy my own needs by controlling the lives of others? Do I have fear/anger issues that cause me to lash out? Jesus is the answer. Jesus alone can give me life, heal my hurts, satisfy my desires, and fill me with the love that drives out all fears. The spear through His side was the stake in the heart of my walking dead flesh. The passions and desires that made me a monster were crucified with Him and buried. In Jesus, there is a real breaking dawn. The Son of righteousness has risen with healing in His wings. He heals the disease. He sets us free from this body of death. He fills us with His love. That's the gospel of Halloween. Healing love is the answer to all of our violent ugly deathliness.

So if you know any monsters, please remember they're already dead. You telling them that they're dead, and that one day the Great Monster Hunter in the sky is coming down to consume their walking corpses with fire may not have the desired effect. Speaking death to dead people is not going to bring life. So speak life. Draw people into the light of Jesus, and do everything you can to show them His love. That's what they really need.

> *For you were called to be free brothers. Only don't use this freedom as an opportunity for the flesh, but serve one another through love. For the entire law is fulfilled in one statement: Love your neighbor as yourself.*

> Galatians 5:13-14

RULES

As Goliath approached, David ran out to meet him and, reaching into his shepherd's bag, took out a stone, and hurled it from his sling, and hit the Philistine in the forehead. The stone sank in, and the man fell on his face to the ground.[104]

was reading a book recently in which the author stated that we have been telling the story of David and Goliath wrong all this time. It's our cultural bias you see—too many epic hero movies with big, tough, intimidating guys in heavy armor crushing their opponents. Both Goliath and Saul expected David to honor the cultural rules and go toe-to-toe with Goliath in a Darwinian bash-off. That was the game that Goliath was playing, and that was the game he was absolutely sure to win. It's why he issues the challenge, "Come to me. . . ." Goliath was big and evidently quite strong. I am aware of the arguments that older, more reliable texts suggests that Goliath was only 6' 9", but that matters very little to me as I have watched a 6' 9" 400-pound man pick up a 1,320-pound log and walk five steps with it. A giant is a giant, and the difference between 6' 9" and 9' 6" is just not significant to me. Based on weight conversions, Goliath's armor weighed between 78 and 125 pounds (the shekel-weight varied from place to place back then), and the head of his spear weighed a minimum of 15 pounds. A little known fact about me is that I have spent a fair amount of time slinging a six-pound splitting maul on the end of a three-foot stick. Therefore, my imagination tells me that it does not really matter if you are wearing armor or not or even if Goliath's spear is sharp or not. If a giant man hits you with a 15-pound hunk of metal mounted on the end of a big stick, it's going to hurt bad. This part we all know. But what we often miss because of our bias is that once David changed the rules of the game, the result was a foregone conclusion; Goliath had absolutely no hope of victory.

Everyone in that day knew that heavy infantry could not stand against slingers. A skilled slinger could, in less than one second, sling a fist-sized stone at about the same speed as a Major League fastball and could do considerable damage from a distance. History tells us that Xenophon's Rhodian slingers could out-range the Persian archers they faced off against. The Romans actually invented a tool to remove sling stones that were lodged in people's bodies.

So let's review briefly. We have one very large, almost stationary man, taken by surprise by a slinger who could easily have stood several hundred feet away and still hit him with a fist-sized rock traveling at over 100 mph. Now ask yourself who actually had the advantage?

Here's the point that I have been considering. Once David changes the rules of the game, all of Goliath's advantages (metal armor, metal weapons, training, experience, size, and strength) become the disadvantages that guarantee his death. The moral of the story: never fight the battle your opponent wants. Change the game, and you change the outcome. David knew the cultural script for this game: two powerful, heavily-armed and armored men bashing at each with swords until one overpowers the other. David knew he had no chance of winning that game, so he simply changed the game. The reality of the new game is that Goliath would have been no worse off if David had been armed with a Colt .45. David could hit Goliath just as far away, just as hard, just as fast, and just as accurately as if he'd had a modern handgun.

So when people, circumstances, or powers come at you with all the intimidating force of a Goliath challenging you to face them on their terms stop and think a moment: Is there a way that you can change the game? Where does that even start? For David, humility had a part to play. He recognized that he had no business suiting up in Saul's armor. He had the humility to see himself as he truly was—absolutely incapable of playing the game as it was being presented to him. David had been anointed king, and here was his first opportunity to do what kings did. If David had let pride push him into the game that people expected him to play, he would have ended up as nothing more than a smear on a spear. How many times have I allowed my own simple, stupid pride to draw me into a game I knew I could not win? (Okay, that was rhetorical, people.)

If you think about everything Jesus did and said, he was all about changing the game: "Do not resist an evil person," "Love your enemy," "Bless those who curse, pray for those despitefully use you." This element is echoed by Paul when he said, "Overcome evil with good." The rule of this world is, "Might makes right," but the rule of God's kingdom is, "Right makes might." In other words, as long as we are right with God, He is able to make all grace abound towards us, and through His power, He has given us all things necessary for life and godliness.

To walk in God's divine power, we have to change the game and play by His rules. We need to put off Saul's armor and refuse to meet Goliath on his own terms.

Colossians 3:8-9 describes some of the weapons and the armor of the world: anger, wrath, malice, slander, filthy language, and deceit. Our old selves know instinctively how to use anger or filthy language as armor to keep others from getting at our inner selves. Our old selves know how to use malice, slander, and deceit as weapons. This is the game that comes naturally to our old selves. It is easy to react automatically to the Goliaths in our lives, and thus, many of us know what it feels like to be nothing more than a smear on a spear.

So how do we change the game? What are the weapons and the armor at our disposal?

> *Therefore, God's chosen ones, holy and loved, put on heartfelt compassion, kindness, humility, gentleness, and patience, accepting one another and forgiving one another if anyone has a complaint against another. Just as the Lord has forgiven you, so you must also forgive. Above all, put on love—the perfect bond of unity. And let the peace of the Messiah, to which you were also called in one body, control your hearts. Be thankful. Let the message about the Messiah dwell richly among you, teaching and admonishing one another in all wisdom, and singing psalms, hymns, and spiritual songs, with gratitude in your hearts to God. And whatever you do, in word or in deed, do everything in the name of the Lord Jesus, giving thanks to God the Father through Him.*

Colossians 3:12-17

It starts with identity, knowing that we are "God's chosen ones holy and loved." As God's chosen ones then, the game is changed from "might makes right" to "right makes might," and God empowers us to armor up with compassion, kindness, humility, gentleness, patience, and peace, and to wield the weapons of righteousness which are acceptance, forgiveness, love, worship, and gratitude. When an angry Goliath challenges you to a bash-off, change the game and respond with love, acceptance, and forgiveness. Learn to stand in God's peace with all gratitude, and worship the God whose eyes "roam throughout the earth to show Himself strong for those whose hearts are completely his."[105]

So remember three things the next time a Goliath steps into your life:

1) Change the game, and you change the outcome.

2) Right makes might

3) God is able to make all grace abound toward you.

Remember that God has already written the playbook for the game we need to be playing.

SADNESS

"Joy in sadness." That's what I heard God say the other day. Now my all-too-human reaction to that was to think, "Oh great. That means there will be sadness." I have to be honest here, yes? Sometimes when God speaks to me, I hear the wrong things. When God says, "Joy in sadness," He is not announcing that there will be sadness. It does not take a prophet to know there will be sadness. God's announcement means there will be joy in sadness. In my mind's eye, I had this picture of a single drop of soap hitting the surface of the water in a dirty pan. You all know what I am talking about? As soon as the soap hits the water, all of the grease that was clouding the surface suddenly pulls back to the edges of the pan, and the surface of the water becomes clear. A single drop of God's joy is enough to bring clarity in the midst of sadness.

We are not immune to sorrow just because we are faithful and faith-filled followers of Jesus. We live in this world, and sadness comes with the territory. Jesus, who was acquainted with sorrow, said:

In this world you have will have trouble, but take heart . . .

John 16:33

I stopped right there on purpose because I think sometimes we need to ask ourselves if we are not more convinced that we will have trouble than we are that He has overcome the world.

I am in the world but not of it. What this means is that while I may have sorrow, sorrow does not have me. Sorrow makes me weak, but I know that when I am weak, then He is strong. Sadness makes me weak, but I know that the joy of the Lord is my strength. His joy is my strength. I think the biggest issue here is that we fail to understand the joy of God. The joy of Jesus is a joy that can look through all of the sorrow and sadness rushing upon Him like a freight train to a greater reality that lies beyond. That's the joy that we need a revelation of.

If you feel like you are living on the thin edge between the kingdom of darkness and the Kingdom of light, may I announce that the word of the Lord to us all is "Joy in sadness." It only takes one drop of His joy to bring clarity in the midst of sadness. So may you today have a revelation of the joy of God. May you experience today the strength of His joy so that you may truly say, "I am in the world but not of it. While I may have sorrow, sorrow does not have me."

TEMPTATIONS

I have heard it said many times in my many decades of church going that we will always have to deal with temptation, especially (as men) sexual temptation. First off, maybe that's just sexist and stupid; secondly, that's not good news. I have been thinking about this for a while and have decided that since God has given us everything required for life and godliness, He must have given us a way to live beyond temptation.

I have also heard it said many, many times that sinning is sin, but being tempted is not. It's just being tempted, so we should not feel bad about being tempted. I hope you will soon see that this idea is not helpful in the pursuit of holiness. The good news is that we can live not only sin-free, but also temptation-free.

James describes the mechanism of temptation for us:

> *Each one is tempted when he is drawn away by his own desires and enticed. Then, when desire has conceived, it gives birth to sin; and sin, when it is full-grown, brings forth death.*

1:14

I see two distinct elements here that we need to address: the issue of being "drawn away," and the issue of our desires. When we address both these issues at the same time, we can move into a place of temptation-free living.

The Greek word which is translated, "drawn away," can be literally translated as "being out drawn" and begs a serious question. What are we being drawn out from? Once again, it is all about presence. In the presence of what or in the presence of whom are you standing? What are you presenting yourself to? That is your choice in any situation, to be present to God or to be present to something or someone else. Paul writes in Romans 6 that if we present (literally, "standing up beside") ourselves to someone to serve them, we become a slave of the person or thing that we obey. So the first key here is that we will serve whatever we are present to. If we are present to fear, it will rule over us. If we are present to God, His peace will guard our hearts and our minds. The question is, will we participate in being drawn out from the presence of God or will we actively make ourselves present to God? The same Greek word "present" (standing up beside) is used both in Romans 6:16 and Romans 12:1:

> *Present your bodies as a living sacrifice, holy and pleasing to God; this is your spiritual worship.*

So we choose in any given moment what we are present to. That's the first key.

The Greek word which is translated, "desire" can be literally translated as "longing," and by implication means a longing for something that is forbidden. Therefore, various English translations render it as, "desires" or "lusts." This is where we have to be brutally honest with ourselves. James says that temptation is the result of being drawn out of the presence of God by our own longings or desires. There is no "the devil made me do it." There is no devil even required. Our own desires are likened to a womb. When opportunity meets desire, something is conceived, which, if allowed to grow, gives birth to sin. That's all temptation really is, opportunity meeting desire. Some opportunities come by mere circumstance, while others are cleverly set up for us via demonic scheming. Regardless, sin is still just an issue of opportunity meeting desire. The struggle that goes on in the heart and mind to not give in to sin actually takes place after conception. It's a struggle precisely because there is already something growing inside of us.

There are two ways to eliminate the struggle: avoid opportunity, or eliminate the desire. I think we instinctively understand the first option, but are often completely blind to the second. In an attempt to live sin-free lives, we set up all kinds of barriers in order to limit opportunity, and thus prevent the conception of sin. Sometimes this works, but sometimes the price is as high as the price of sin itself as people can become rigidly and even bitterly legalistic in their efforts to prevent opportunity. Barrier methods are not perfect, and unwanted conceptions still happen. Instead of just trying to limit opportunity, what if we focus instead on changing our desires? Again, it is all about presence.

> *Delight yourself in the Lord, and he will give you*
> *the desires of your heart.*

> Psalm 37:4

When being present to God becomes the main thing in our lives and we learn to delight in Him, our desires will change. When our desires change, they will all be met. When all of our desires are met in Christ, there will simply be no womb for temptation in our lives.

How do we put this into practice? Proactively we need to make the presence of God the main thing in everything. Not that there is ever any lack in His presence, the fault is always in our own lack of presence. We need to be constantly checking in, constantly reordering our thoughts, making sure that we are being present to God as the priority of our being, **and** we need to be constantly delighting in His presence. In this way, our desires will change. Remember, whatever we present ourselves to will rule over us. When we present ourselves to God, it His desires that rule over us until our desires become His, and we are completely satisfied in Him. This is an intentional not an accidental process:

> Set your mind on things above, not on earthly things.[106]

> Walk by the Spirit and you will not carry out the desire of the flesh.[107]

> Present your bodies as a living sacrifice, holy and pleasing to God . . . [108]

Reactively, we need to change the way we think. Remember that temptation is opportunity meeting our own desires. This means that temptation is an indication that there are ungodly desires that need to be rooted out of our hearts. If I am being tempted, it is because I have a longing for something that is not godly, and I am being present to that longing rather than being present to the fullness of Christ in me. So I can resist the desire that is drawing me out of the presence of God, or I can press into the Presence, confess the temptation to God as evidence of desires in me that are not aligned with His, and ask Him to create in me a clean heart and renew a right spirit within me. Am I saying that confession and healing are necessary even when I have not yet yielded to temptation and actually sinned? Yes, that is exactly what I am saying. Confession, repentance, and healing are not just for the sinner; they are for every true saint who wants to honor the holiness of a God who has made a way for us to live beyond temptation.

VANITY

Thou shalt not take the name of the LORD thy God
in vain . . .

Exodus 20:7, KJV

am so guilty. That's the problem with revelation, you know. Sometime it is encouraging, releasing, and wonderful, and sometimes it smacks you between the eyes with a big ol' 2x4 of "Now what?" You see, I had a revelation. There is more to this passage—much more—than whether or not we curse or make/take oaths in God's name. It is devastatingly simple, and once I saw it, I realized how guilty I have been.

One word is the key: the word that we translate "take."[109] It has a variety of meanings and could be translated more precisely as "take up," "carry," or even "bear." The primary meaning of the Aramaic word which most closely corresponds to the Hebrew means to "carry."

In a traditional Western marriage, when a woman marries a man, she takes his name. She now bears or carries his name instead of the one she was born with. Now let's consider for a moment if this woman continued to live like she was single after she was married; not accepting her husband's affection and devotion, not sharing in the work he is doing in the world, but instead giving her attention to others. She now carries his name but she is not living the life that goes with the name. She is neither receiving the benefits of taking his name nor bearing up to the responsibilities of taking his name. His name means nothing in her life. She has taken his name in vain.

The elder brother in the story of the prodigal son is another example. He was told, "You are always with me, and everything I have is yours," but he missed it because, like the fictional woman above, he carried his father's name in vain.

I was born with one name, but now because of His great love, I carry His. But, oh, how often do I carry that name in vain? If I am anxious about paying my bills, then I have taken up His name in vain. If I cultivate my frustration in the face of His peace, then I have taken up His name in vain. If I live in fear in the face of His love, then I have taken His name in vain. I have taken up the name of the Creator of all who gives life to the dead and speaks of things that are not as if they were. If I fail from fear, ignorance, or apathy to speak a word of life, to pray for someone's healing, or to give to someone in need, then I have taken up His name in vain. If I have taken His name but continue to live in this world as if nothing has changed, then I have taken His name in vain. It's just that simple. If I fail to appropriate the benefits of taking His name or fail to live out the responsibilities of taking His name, then I have taken His name in vain. And so I find after all these years of carrying His name that something has to change lest I find myself continuing to take His name in vain.

I was going to end this by saying that this malady touches so many areas of my life, that I do not even know where to begin to make changes. But God has a generous sense of humor. A friend called a few minutes ago because his son broke his foot, and he wants prayer for healing. So that's where I am going to start. Not because I'm special, anointed, or even feel particularly full of faith, but because I have taken His name and I will no longer carry it in vain.

YES

For the Son of God, Jesus Christ . . . did not become "Yes and no"; on the contrary, a final "Yes" has come in Him. For every one of God's promises is "Yes" in Him. Therefore, the "Amen" is also spoken through Him by us for God's glory.

2 Corinthians 1:19, 20

One of the more significant shifts in my thinking has been to realize that God is the God of "yes." When God created the heavens and earth, it was an expression of the divine "yes"—an invitation to enter into the joy of God expressed in the love of the perfect Father, the obedience of the beloved Son, and the fellowship of the loving Spirit.

When God chose a people for Himself, He spoke over them a divine "yes." We read it like a list of "no's" because that's how it comes across—"thou shalt not"—but we need to learn to see this as God's divine "yes." We need to understand that this list that we think of as "no's" was spoken to a people whom God was calling out of the world to experience His presence and His glory and to reflect that glory back into the world from which they had been drawn out. At the time, they were a "not-people" who were enslaved and oppressed by both men and gods. They lived in fear, struggling day after unchanging day with no rest and no hope. Then God comes along with what appears to be "no's" by which He is actually saying, "Yes, you can live a different way. Yes, you can live without fear of the gods of Egypt or Canaan or America (or wherever you live). Yes, you can know the Creator of the universe by name. Yes, you can live satisfied with who you are and what you have. Yes, you can live at peace with your parents, your wife, and your neighbors. Yes you can live whole. Just learn to say, 'yes' to Me, and all these things will be yours."

Like the Hebrews, we, too, once lived in the kingdom of darkness where we were enslaved, oppressed, dissatisfied; we were without rest and without hope. Now we have been brought into the Kingdom of His glorious Son where all is "Yes!"

It is a tragedy for us to believe that the secret of piety or of holiness lies in saying "no" to the things of the kingdom we have been brought out of. What do I have to do with that kingdom any longer? The secret of holy living lies not in saying "no" to the things that are passing away, but in saying "yes" to the Kingdom in which we now live and is yet coming upon us. Jesus is the final "yes," and all the promises of God are "yes" in Him and in Christ, we say "amen" to His "yes." In other words, we need to come into agreement with Him. We need to say "yes" to His "yes." That is the secret to living in the Kingdom of God.

All of sin can be summarized as simply this: saying "no" in the face of God's "yes." All of holiness can be summarized as simply this: saying "yes" in the face of God's "yes." Let me challenge you with this thought. If you are struggling in any area of your life, consider for a moment if you are trying to live out of a "no." Are you living a self-controlling life of saying "no" because you think that's what it takes to make God happy? Living out of a "no" to the things of this world will constrain some behaviors and give the appearance of godliness, but "no" lacks the power to give life. Instead, ask the Holy Spirit to help you find God's "yes" in your life. Look for it. Search for it as you would a hidden treasure; then when you find it, embrace it with everything you are.

For those of you are who are simply holding out on God, living a self-limiting life because you are afraid of the cost of saying "yes," it's time to learn to think a different way.

I hope that as you have come to the end of this book you have picked up on the theme of the Now. There is a Now-ness to the Kingdom of God. There is Now-ness to the glory of God, the peace of God, the happiness of God, the desire of God, etc. If you haven't heard this yet through reading this book, **now** is the time to stop putting off for Someday the things that God has for you Today.

And all it takes to step into the NOW of God is for you to say, "yes" to the next thing.

End Notes

Vision
[1] See Matt 6:33.
[2] See Phil 4:19.
[3] See Rom 5:8.
[4] See Dan 9:5.
[5] See Rom 8:15.
[6] See 1 Cor 2:12, John 16:13, and 1 Cor. 3:18-23.
[7] See 2 Tim 1:7.
[8] See Rom 5:5.
[9] See 1 Cor 2:16.
[10] See 1 Cor 4:1.

Treasure
[11] See John 6:63.
[12] See Mal 4:5, 6.

Lost?
[13] NKJV.
[14] See Phil 2:6.

Promise
[15] Burge, Gary. *The Bible and the Land*, Zondervan, 2009.
[16] See Rom 1:17.
[17] See Dr. Burge's book, *The Bible and the Land* for more on this.

Answers
[18] See 1 Kings 17:2-6.

Disappointment
[19] See 1 Cor 13:7.
[20] See 1 John 4:8.

[21] See Gen 3:6.
[22] See Exod 15:26.

Believing

[23] "Holy Spirit," Bryan Torwalt and Katie Torwalt, ©2011 Jesus Culture (Admin. by Jesus Culture Music).
[24] See Heb 10:20.
[25] See Phil 3:14.
[26] See Eph 2:10, 3:20; 1 Cor 29.
[27] "I'll Fly Away," by Albert E. Brumley ©1929, published in 1932 by Hartford Music Company.

Happiness

[28] "Blessed Assurance," lyrics written by Fanny Cosby in 1873; music written by Phoebe Knapp in 1873.

Mystery

[29] See James 4:1-3.
[30] See Matt 6:33.
[31] See Rom 5:8.

Between

[32] See Acts 1:6.
[33] See John 2:4.
[34] Luke 17:21.

Breathe

[35] *The Unvarnished New Testament: A New Translation From the Original Greek,* translated by Andy Gaus. Publisher: Phanes Press, Grand Rapids, MI, 1991.
[36] Gen 2:7, *The Unvarnished NT,* emphasis added..
[37] Matt 3:11, *The Unvarnished NT,* emphasis added.
[38] *The Unvarnished NT.,* p 77, emphasis added.
[39] *The Unvarnished NT,* p 175, emphasis added
[40] *The Unvarnished NT,* p 174, emphasis added
[41] Matt 10:17, emphasis added
[42] *The Unvarnished NT,* p 212, emphasis added.
[43] *The Unvarnished NT,* p 229, emphasis added.
[44] Eph 5:19, emphasis added.

Binary

[45] See Josh 5:13, 14.

[46] See John 8:11.
[47] See John 9:2, 3.
[48] See Luke 20:22.
[49] See Matt 14:15.
[50] See Matt 14:31.
[51] Isa 30:21.

But . . .

[52] American Television game show, "Jeopardy!"® hosted by, Alex Trebek.
[53] See John 17.
[54] See Col 2:9.
[55] See John 1:14.
[56] See John 1:16.

Thermostats

[57] "Wherever We Go", Newsboys, copyright ©2006, ©2009 Inpop Records. Manufactured by EMI Christian Music Group, ©2009 Inpop Records.

Kingsmen

[58] The Unvarnished NT.

Companions

[59] See Rom 8:14.
[60] See John 14:9
[61] See Jonn 14:17.
[62] See John 14:26.
[63] See John 16:15.

Dying

[64] See 2 Cor 5:8.

Enough

[65] See James 4:2-3.

Prosperity

[66] See 2 Cor 9:10.
[67] See Matt 6:25.

Exceeding
[68] See John 3:34.

Ergonomics
[69] Exod 3:2.
[70] Eph 2:10.
[71] See Eph 4:12 and 2 Tim 3:17.
[72] See 2 Tim 4:5.
[73] See Matt 3:16-17 and Luke 4:18.
[74] See Matt 28:19.
[75] See Acts 1:4, 8.
[76] See Eph 1:19.
[77] Sourced from scripture4all.org
[78] See Eph 3:16.
[79] See Eph 3:19.

Us
[80] See Matt 6:11-13, emphasis added.

Mercy
[81] See Heb 4:16.
[82] See Mark 10:47.
[83] See v 51.
[84] See Heb 4:16.

Grace
[85] John 1:14, HCSB.
[86] John 1:16, HCSB.
[87] Col 2:9
[88] See John 1:18, 14:9.
[89] See James 1:17.

Healing
[90] Tolkien, J.R.R. *The Return of the King.* Published by George Allen & Unwin, 1955, UK.
[91] See Exod 15:6.
[92] See Matt 1:21.

Hope
[93] See Rom 5:5.
[94] Prov 13:12.

Glory
[95] Exod 33:18
[96] See John 17.
[97] See Eph 2.
[98] See John 17:3.

Kedging
[99] See Rom 5:5.

Now
[100] See Isa 9:7.
[101] Luke 2:14.
[102] See Luke 4.

Legacy
[103] Eccl 12:6

Rules
[104] See 1 Sam 17 for the full story.
[105] 2 Chron 16:9.

Temptations
[106] Col 3:2.
[107] Gal 5:16, HCSB.
[108] Rom 12:1, HCSB.

Vanity
[109] *Strong's Concordance*, #H5375 (*nasa*).

75477085R00123

Made in the USA
Columbia, SC
18 August 2017